Building China:
Studies in Integrated Development

Building China:
Studies in Integrated Development

Edited by John F. Jones

The Chinese University Press
Hong Kong

International Standard Book Number: 962-201-208-6

The Chinese University Press
SHATIN, N.T., HONG KONG

Published with a grant from the Social Welfare and
Development Centre for Asia and the Pacific.

Typesetting by The Chinese University Press
Printing by Wing Tai Cheung Printing Co. Ltd.

Contents

Contents

Preface

The Social Welfare and Development Centre for Asia and the Pacific was established in Manila, Philippines, in 1976, as an intergovernmental research and training institution, assisted by the United Nations Development Programme under the auspices of the United Nations Economic and Social Commission for Asia and the Pacific. The following developmental objectives of SWDCAP identify four major processes crucial to the attainment of comprehensive development:

Socio-economic integration: bringing together the necessary processes and components of social and economic institutions, in a proper balance, to achieve the progressive development of society.

Institution development: a process of creative dialectics between change agents and their target groups to promote self-reliance and a supportive, self-actualizing network of institutions and values.

Structural change: changes in values, social institutions and patterns of societal relationships brought about by a restructuring of roles and/or a re-allocation of resources.

Evaluation: constant reassessment of programmes and change measures to ensure their continued relevance in the context of development.

The operationalization of these objectives is mainly done through the following tasks in the Asian and Pacific countries:

(a) studies of social welfare policies;
(b) research into the urban and rural aspects of development with special reference to migration and resettlement, women's role, child development, family planning, nutrition and primary health care;
(c) training for social policy tasks;
(d) training for implementing social programmes aimed at enhancing national development efforts;
(e) publications related to the above areas.

With reference to the last effort, SWDCAP not only publishes the results of its own studies, research and related workshops but also encourages and sponsors the publications of others which throw more light on the processes of development, particularly in regard to the social dimensions. Not only do the social aspects of development come under our scope of study and training, but also *economic* development itself, since among other things, its main objective is to promote *social development*. It is in this context that the present volume is presented.

The articles selected for publication represent measures to transform Chinese society. The Introduction stresses the significance and difficulties of this task when discussing the concept of integrated development. The chapter on "Factors Accounting for China's Early Success in Industrialization" is interesting in as much as it tries to show how the resources of the country are geared towards the goals of promoting the welfare of the people. The implementation of the development effort is largely done through organizations, hence the relevance of "In Defense of Bureaucracy" which describes the de-radicalisation of Maoism as a prelude to the modernization of the country. More directly concerned with the social aspects of development, "The Development of Rural Health Care" highlights a programme of great significance among welfare measures. The chapter examines the role of two rather critical social infrastructures: the medical system and the commune. Education, another important social measure, is also discussed in the context of the commune, and the link between a micro society's needs and macro level national policies is perhaps best illustrated here. Finally, we are given an opportunity to learn about one crucial aspect of the country's efforts at development—the way people organize, and are organized, to carry out the development tasks. The article on water conservation is a good illustration of the mobilization of people for development.

While it is the authors who are solely responsible for the content of the chapters, we in SWDCAP would like to invite the attention of the readers to the experience of China and its implications for social development in other countries. The Chinese University of Hong Kong is a neighbour of mainland China and has therefore been in a position to observe, study and document the transformation that has been taking place in the People's Republic of China. The series of studies presented to the reader document an important effort at development which has significance for students of human welfare.

SWDCAP would like to record the initiative and enthusiasm of Professor John F. Jones, Chairman of the Social Work Department of The Chinese University of Hong Kong. It was indeed an enriching and exciting experience for SWDCAP staff to work closely with Professor Jones in this scholarly endeavour.

AHMAD FATTAHIPOUR
Director
Social Welfare and Development Centre
for Asia and the Pacific

Introduction

Integrated development remains as elusive as Utopia itself and no nation (certainly not China) can claim to have mastered its secret perfectly. The right mix of social, economic and political factors which add up to balanced progress is found in books—and occasionally Five-Year Plans—rather than in the real world of people to which even economists and politicians belong. Yet, for all its will-of-the-wisp qualities, unified development is clearly preferable to a hit-and-miss approach in building a country and, for that if for no other reason, planners and, in a less conscious way perhaps, ordinary citizens long for a way to harness individual efforts and bring together diverse plans for the good of all. The process of unification as well as the result—where it is achieved—can be called integrated development.

The process starts every time a country or its leaders decide on a new direction which demands a concentrated, national effort. Of course, the call for unity does not guarantee unity, and unity itself may amount to nothing more than a wish to build a great republic, without actually doing it. Still, the idea of progress is captivating enough to attract most people, so that probably the majority of countries at least hanker after integrated development. National prestige is at stake.

Besides national prestige, there is another reason why we might expect integrated development to rank high as a goal among a select number of countries. Whenever a revolution occurs—whether religious, secular, economic or social, whether popular or engineered by a few—there is invariably house cleaning. The old order must go; the new emerge. Because revolutions are radical, they aim to change society at its roots. In plain terms, this usually means subordinating personal objectives and institutional purposes to a grand design. It also means choosing strategies that promote a dream. In the Chinese revolution the aim was no less than the creation of "a new person," "the socialist man." To this end, the means of government, the economy, the social infrastructures such as education, and the very environment were reworked. Furthermore, the intention was, in sociological jargon, that the different bureaucracies and primary groups (neighbors and families) should function together with the common goal of building the new China. The various shifts of policy and the recent disavowal of extremism signified by the overthrow of the Gang of Four means that the ideal was not fully attained. But the goal of the Chinese revolution was unified development, and it remains so today.

What is integrated, or (the adjectives are interchangeable) unified, development? Before studying the Chinese experience, it is necessary to explore the nature of development so that we may have some yardstick to measure progress. Examining integrated development, it is possible to discern two main processes which, under political pressure, coalesce: economic progress and social betterment. Each process has a cluster of sub-processes which may come about in different sequences and at different speeds, but together economic and social advancement are responsible for structural change in a society. Briefly, economic progress can be defined as a structural transformation of the economy by which those mechanisms that are functionally required for sustained growth are permanently incorporated into the economy. Social betterment, the ultimate goal of development, at first sight seems self-explanatory until we reflect on its complexity. While basic human needs—for food, shelter, and so on—are simple enough to understand, the definition of social betterment which is nationally accepted will depend on what the total population or a significant part of it considers best—and for whom. The definition, therefore, is likely to change; yet most people have an instinctive grasp of the meaning of social progress. The U. N. General Assembly, stressing the importance of the social component, declared (in its usual general fashion) that the essence of development was:

(a) to leave no sector of the population outside the scope of change and development,
(b) to effect structural change which favors national development and to activate all sectors of the population to participate in the development process,
(c) to aim at social equity, including the achievement of an equitable distribution of income and wealth in the nation,
(d) to give high priority to the development of human potential, including vocational and technical training, the provision of employment opportunities and meeting the needs of children.[1]

The meshing of the economic and social components in development is largely determined by national policies which in turn reflect a political ideal. Myrdal alludes to this when he places "policies" last in a series of categories meant to describe the economic and non-economic conditions of development. The conditions, causally interrelated, are:

(1) outputs and incomes;
(2) conditions of production;
(3) levels of living;
(4) attitudes towards life and work;
(5) institutions;
(6) policies.[2]

[1] The text of the General Assembly Resolution 2681 (XXV) can be found in *International Social Development Review*, No. 3 (1971).

[2] Gunnar Myrdal, *Asian Drama* (Harmondsworth: Penguin Books, 1968), Vol. III, Appendix 2, pp. 1859-1860.

Policies generally embody the values and preferences of the dominant social forces of a country. Another way of putting this is to say that policies signify "the preferred style of development" in contrast to "the real style" which is empirically observable in the levels and structures of production, the participation of different classes in economic, social and political activities, the distribution of wealth, the patterns of consumption, etc. The preferred style is what the national political leadership, the administrative planning units, or a significant portion of the population would like to see happen. Depending on the propaganda devices available, and the clarity with which proponents articulate their thoughts, the preferred style may be proclaimed from the rooftops or seen in a glass darkly. (Some of the coded messages in Chinese public statements might suggest to outsiders that a way has been found to do both at the same time.) Very often the official version of the preferred style will be modified in practice by those who challenge government policy.

National policy requires a series of political decisions relating to (a) national autonomy, (b) the extent of popular participation, (c) individual security and freedom, (d) the emphasis given to production in general as well as to production techniques and controls in particular, (e) mechanisms for the distribution of benefits, (f) the individual or collective consumption of goods and services, (g) the protection of the human environment, and (h) the safeguarding of group solidarity.[3]

Listing the necessary political decisions is easy enough, the hard part is to shape a consistent policy so that sectoral plans are mutually supportive rather than the reverse. The objective always is to integrate. But planning has what might almost be called a divisive component in that it is necessary to tackle any project piece by piece. Comprehensive planning is not a single operation but is further divided into financial planning, resource or allocative planning, physical planning and institutional planning. It can be seen that the obstacles to unified development multiply with the plans. In reality, of course, political leaders, bureaucrats, particular interest groups and factions of one sort or another try to foist their ideas on the rest and employ tactics meant to convince or coerce others. The contending parties may have only a limited grasp of their opponents' viewpoint, and as little concern. Decision-making tends to be a seesaw of conflict and consensus, pressure and negotiation until one side gets ahead and can dictate terms. National plans will vary widely in their coherence or diffuseness, their compatibility or incompatibility with preferred styles of development, but they always constitute a political process stemming

[3]Commission for Social Development, Economic and Social Council, *Report on a Unified Approach to Development Analysis and Planning* (New York: United Nations, 1972), p. 14.

from the distribution of power at the regional, national, and indeed international levels.

Because integrated development is so global, the only hope of achieving it lies in the selection of strategies. A strategy attempts to make a preferred style of development real by proposing concrete decisions and priorities, with specifications of the means, the resource allocations, and the necessary institutional changes. A strategy is not the same thing as a development plan—many countries have clear strategies for development without the benefit of Five-Year Plans, while others have national plans which are too fuzzy to be called strategic. Integrated development requires the presence of an authentic strategy which takes full account of the existing style of development, warts and all, and seeks to bring it closer to the preferred style. It requires an awareness of the objective constraints that hamper the implementation of policy.

Most nations have only a limited number of strategies open to them, and the choice of these will depend on aspirations for rapid progress, popular adherence to tradition, as well as the strength of the elite either favoring or frowning upon change. Strategies are not always successful, occasionally because wrong assumptions are made about their consequences. Following a socialist revolution, for instance, the leaders may reject the primacy of market forces and material incentives, seeking instead to combat private ownership or consumption demands that conflict with the preferred (idealistic) style of development. The leaders may assume that increased production is very compatible with state ownership, and expect production to soar with the re-education of the masses—while still not making production the chief aim. In such instances, the goal of the revolution is primarily egalitarian, and production objectives are not allowed to override the central purpose of the new society. However, the rising aspirations of the people, their impatience with sacrifice, in addition perhaps to the demands of the military for a strong, industrial base, may bring about alterations in the preferred style. The fact is, few societies are able to pursue their version of Utopia in a completely consistent manner over a long period of time. Contradictions appear and adjustments must be made.

Three strategic orientations are particularly important in a unified approach to national planning; they relate to the comprehensiveness, the rapidity and the distribution of development.[4] Without attention to these general areas, socio-economic development tends to be spotty at best.

A development strategy must be as universal as possible so that the entire society is covered. Planning should start from a comprehensive assessment of complementary and alternative ways of reaching national goals. It should aim

[4] *Ibid.*, pp. 22-24.

at peak efficiency in the use of scarce resources—not only capital but motivated and trained manpower. The scope of the development strategy should extend to the total population rather than a section of it, like the army, the civil service, the party or, more broadly perhaps, the urban communities.

Undoubtedly, the most telling argument in favor of strategies which promote rapid development is the fact that mass poverty ought not to be tolerated. Unfortunately, the argument is sometimes twisted to suggest that economic expansion is the first priority, ignoring the evidence that hunger and unemployment can exist side by side with a relatively prosperous economy. The excuse is sometimes given that a particular nation must first "catch up" with developed countries and can postpone tackling social problems. The cost to a national society of such a policy can be great. Those who do not share in development become its first victims. Rapid development, therefore, is necessary not just for one sector or for one elite group, but across the board. It is all the more crucial because of the inertia of national institutions which allow small incremental changes without altering the structure of society. For this reason, too, the development effort must be dramatic enough to capture the key actors and the masses for united action.

A declaration of rights gives no assurance that the benefits of development will reach everyone. Nor does the enactment of "universal coverage" automatically make services available to those who need them most. Typically, in any social system, services as well as income tend to be most satisfactory for those holding power in society. The powerless get least. The problem of distribution, then, is not so much a question of establishing a guaranteed minimum income (although a country does well to define its poverty level below which none must fall) as it is the reapportionment of power and control over production and distribution. Consumer demand should be met in some equitable fashion, and that requires more than declaring what the lowest acceptable standard of living is. Generally it calls for calculated intervention in the social process and discrimination in favor of the disadvantaged.

Moving down from general strategic orientations towards comprehensiveness, rapidity and distribution, a government must evolve concrete strategies to deal with sectoral policy problems. A tactical approach is necessary in the areas of rural development, industrialization, employment, health care, education, population and the physical environment. Ideally, these strategies should be interrelated so that they lead to balanced progress. The Chinese formulation "to walk on two legs," referring to development, is appropriate in this context. Nations which have concentrated on urban industrialization, for instance, while ignoring the needs of the majority of the people living in the countryside have usually exploited the rural population by taking much and giving little. It is ironic that in many parts of Asia those engaged in agriculture enjoy the lowest nutrition levels. Again ideally, the strategies for integrated development should be focused enough and sufficiently selective to encourage a concentration of effort. For example, an education program may be too diffuse to train experts needed for modernization.

There is a temptation to assume that because integrated development requires coordination, all planning should be centralized in a national planning office. This is not so. On the contrary, planning ought to be a widespread activity involving a multitude of agencies, regions, and localities. The notion of a single national plan which takes care of every problem and foresees each eventuality is illusionary. A national plan has a place in the scheme of development provided it does not take over responsibility for decision making at all levels. A national plan gives direction. It does not follow that regional plans are simply miniatures of the original. The tendency of central planners to wish regional or sectoral plans to be reduced scale models of the national plan neglects geographical differences and pays scant attention to the ability of people outside the capital to plan for themselves.

But planning has to be coordinated, nonetheless. It cannot be so erratic that the objectives attached to the sectors of planning activity—industry, agriculture, housing, education, and so on—are viewed as conflicting, and competition for funds becomes catch-as-catch-can. In practice, this always happens to some degree, but the worst effects of competitiveness can be avoided by cross-sectoral planning. Cross-sectoral planning is the core of integrated development. If balanced socio-economic progress is to occur, certain policies ought to be defined as cross-sectoral from the beginning. The selection of these policies should be based on their strategic importance. Key issues are picked out and resources combined to solve problems which no single sector can tackle alone. It may be—to take one example—that, by concentrating on agriculture, unemployment and mass poverty are thereby reduced. A policy favoring higher investments in agriculture has obvious implications for housing, education and industry so that these, too, become the object of cross-sectoral analysis. Another approach to cross-sectoral planning is to identify target groups, i.e., population groups in special need of a variety of services to bring them into the mainstream of society. Whatever approach is taken to cross-sectoral planning, the process demands a management information system coordinating the analysis of the component elements of development.

There is no single index of integrated development which poses a problem when assessing the effectiveness of measures intended to promote it at the national level. Yet some criteria are needed so that at least a tentative judgment can be made as to whether a country such as China has achieved a unified approach. Perhaps for our purposes this can best be done by first summarizing the generic meanings of integrated development. It should then be possible to conclude in what sense or senses China's progress fits the concept of integration.

Development can be integrated in several respects: First, it can be comprehensive in design, a question of scope. Problems and solutions are viewed comprehensively, addressing their political, economic, and social implications. Second, integrated development may mean coordinated change, largely a question of timing. Policy changes, for instance, are integrated when they occur in an orderly manner, either at the same time, or following a planned sequence. Third, development may be integrated vertically, that is, the center and provincial (or local) levels work together on the same policy, with the lower levels following central directives. Fourth, development can be integrated horizontally, with units at the same level cooperating to define and solve problems and to implement policies. Finally, *policy* can be integrated in any of the above senses, while its *implementation* is not.

The complexity of integrated development effectively rules out any claim by a particular nation that it has achieved, once and for all, balanced progress. The most that can realistically be hoped for is partial success. Yet the effort to unify socio-economic planning must go forward, if only because its laissez-faire alternative is too costly. And partial success is worth knowing about; indeed, even failure has a lesson to teach, when demonstrated. There is need to document and collect approaches to unified development at regional and national levels. It is in this context that the People's Republic of China is offered as an illustration.

Why China?

The possible explanations for studying China are many and varied, ranging from neglect in the past to inquisitiveness about the future, but the reasons motivating this work are four in particular.

(1) Studies on socio-economic development in East Asia and the Pacific have failed to pay sufficient attention to China, partly perhaps because of the want of factual data. The United Nations' *1974 Report on the World Social Situation* had this to say:. "China, with an estimated population of some 800 million . . . represents more than 40 per cent of the population of developing countries in the region. In spite of its pre-eminent size and importance, the social situation in China has not been analysed in the present report because of the lack of available information."[5] Into the vacuum created by the scarcity of reliable data came, too often, a mishmash of comment pro and contra China based on propaganda or prejudice. The recent opening of China to outsiders as well as the reappraisal by the Chinese themselves of the past decades have remedied that situation to a considerable

[5]Department of Economic and Social Affairs, *1974 Report of the World Social Situation* (New York: United Nations, 1975), p. 77.

degree, allowing a more realistic assessment of China's progress.

(2) The United Nations has begun to offer the People's Republic of China, now a member of the U.N. system, technical assistance and other services. Knowledge pertaining to China's perspective on development, its preferred style and its strategies for progress is important to those called upon to provide assistance, and indeed to all who are interested in problems of development.

(3) The downfall of the notorious "Gang of Four" marks the end of a political era in China, so it is possible to study China's progress prior to the recent modernization period as a distinct stage of development. This is not to imply that the pre-modernization phase was uniform in its implementation of Maoism or that Maoism itself was without its policy wobbles. But we are probably safe in assuming that the death of Mao and the overthrow of his more radical interpreters mark a turning point in Chinese socialist history.

(4) China's experiment in socio-economic development is founded on Marx-Leninism and Maoist principles. As such, its historical significance is great. Because the government has been self-consciously socialist in its orienta-tion, that ideology would seem to suggest a unified approach to development, in a political sense at least. Whether the Chinese formula for integrated development is good for everyone, more particularly the developing countries, is a matter of judgment. Although there is no homogeneity within the Third World, China undoubtedly shared many common denominators with under-developed countries when it set about its revolution, and offers a unique illustration, if not a model, of socio-economic advancement.

The chapters in *Building China* are what the sub-title says, *Studies in Inte-grated Development*. In no way are they intended to present the full profile of China. Nevertheless, taken together, they offer a sketch of China which hopefully can benefit the scholar, student, and general reader alike. The concept of integrated development can help to liberate planners as well as scholars from such stereotype terminologies as "planned economy" or "central planning" which often conjure up muddy ideas. To look at China's modernization process from this perspective also offers a comprehensive way of understanding and evaluating the Chinese system.

The book makes rather extensive use of on-going research on Guangdong Province communes. Since the summer of 1976, the Social Research Centre of The Chinese University of Hong Kong has been undertaking field studies of several rural communes. The project entitled, "The Commune and Socio-economic Development in Communist China" is an ambitious one and covers most aspects of rural life. The research team has produced a series of research reports on industrial and agricultural enterprises, manpower mobilization, and social services. Selected for this book are three studies focusing on medical care, water conservancy and school education in some of the communes.

The theme of China's integrated development lends itself to systematic examination. The intention, manifest in the Table of Contents, is first to present a general view of China's progress since 1949, then narrow the focus somewhat to more concrete areas (including the commune studies) before ending with a look back at Maoism and the recent revisions. But there is nothing sacred about the sequence and the reader may well choose to follow his own whim rather than the editor's when deciding on the order of reading. To make the choice easier, brief abstracts of the chapters are presented below.

CHAPTER I presents a chronological review of the major changes in China since 1949. According to Jones and Burns, the success of the People's Republic in achieving unified progress has been uneven. Policy makers have adopted a comprehensive perspective, and have coordinated problem-solving in the political, economic and social arenas. But, particularly in the countryside, some policies have tended to undermine horizontal integration. In addition, the disruptions of the Great Leap Forward and the Cultural Revolution seriously affected the organization of central planning and thus reduced vertical integration. Post-1969 developments indicate that many of these problems have been overcome.

CHAPTER II analyzes the success of China's industrialization. Hsueh and Liu compare the paths to industrialization before and after 1949 so that the factors accounting for the success can be identified. These factors include the rationalization of economic behavior by the collective forces, mass mobilization and better utilization of labor, etc. Since China's industrialization has not been uneventful and uniformly successful, the authors also discuss some negative factors associated with China's development.

CHAPTER III explores crucial problem areas in educational policy and discusses the implementation of policy in the context of China's emphasis on agricultural development. These problem areas include the need to close the rural-urban gap, to integrate theory and practice, and to strike a balance between "redness" and "expertness." Ng examines the significance of these in shaping rural education in relation to the people's commune as the basic model of rural development in China. The chapter, like the two following it, uses data drawn from the study of several communes in Guangdong Province.

CHAPTER IV discusses the strategies of developing and organizing health care services in the rural communes of China. Lee and Tsui point out some of the ways in which the political-administrative structure of the rural commune is conducive to the development of both preventive and curative health services.

CHAPTER V, making special reference to water conservation schemes in Guangdong Province, examines the general policy concerning water conservation—

"The lifeline of agriculture." Chan discusses how the construction of various projects was realized under the limitations imposed by the scarcity of capital, machinery, materials, etc. He also states the consequences of the conservation schemes for rural development.

CHAPTER VI is a survey of the Chinese economy after the Cultural Revolution and up to 1976 when Chairman Mao died and the Gang of Four was purged. The major focus is on the goals of the Chinese leadership and the problems encountered—goals and problems shared by many developing countries today. According to Cheng, the Chinese experience was probably unique in that the Chinese leadership not only aimed at promoting economic growth, but also tried to reduce, if not eliminate, the "three big gaps"—the differences in living standards between rural and urban areas, between peasants and industrial workers, and between those doing manual work and those doing mental work. During this period, emphasis was given to the Maoist ideals of self-reliance and molding the new socialist man.

CHAPTER VII analyzes one of the most outstanding phenomena of the Four Modernizations movement of China, namely, bureaucracy. Anti-bureaucratism, which was intended to combat the alleged deradicalizing tendency of the revolution, was the legacy of the Cultural Revolution. However, after the downfall of the Gang of Four, a new idealogy defending the bureaucratic system has emerged. Now, under overriding objective of modernization in general and increasing productivity in particular, Communist China is launching a nation-wide campaign to repudiate radical Maoism which, according to King, placed emphasis on revolutionary romanticism and mass activism. Today, the modernist Maoists are advocating the value of bureaucratic organization of a Weberian kind, which sees hierarchy and professional expertise as essential elements of organization. The modernist elites of Communist China seem to agree with Weber that in the process of transition from the "kingdom of necessity" to the "kingdom of liberty" bureaucraey as a form a rational organization is indispensable, be it in a capitalist or socialist system.

CHAPTER VIII summarizes the contributions of the various authors in relation to key aspects of integrated development. It is a review of China's approach to development as well as an assessment of the nation's success in reaching its goals.

Having synopsized the chapters, a few editorial remarks are pertinent. In a work such as *Building China* it is inevitable that among the authors opinions differ. Interpretation forms a large part of scholarship; subjective judgment is required even to analyze computer data. Where the evidence is incomplete or ambiguous, consensus is hardest. While an editor may be tempted to sympathize with those who, for unity's sake, would impose a party line on scholars, this one had no stomach for the task. Therefore the reader may detect from chapter to chapter different slants, biases and even conclusions. But that, after all, is the nature of open enquiry.

A small but tricky problem when seeking consensus concerns the romanization of Chinese characters. China's attempt at modernization has in the course of the past decades affected the transliteration of Chinese personal names, places and the like—even the spelling of slogans. If the changes were universally recognized and accepted, there would be no problem, but this is a period of transition in letters no less than leaders so that consistency is not to be expected. The present book has its share of idiosyncrasies in that popular English spellings, Wade-Giles romanization, and the Pin-yin of the mainland rub schoulders in its pages. The rationale for allowing a hundred words to bloom is the unfamiliarity to many readers of old names spelled in a new way, the reluctance of authors to have their linguistic conventions tampered with (especially where their work forms part of a larger series of monographs, reports and articles, as in the case of the Guangdong communes studies), and the plain mulishness of people determined to spell right. Editorial prerogative was exercised in adopting uniform spelling for well-known geographical places and political leaders, e.g., Peking and Mao Tse-tung. Otherwise, writers were left to their own devices. A glossary of Chinese words used in the text, with alternative spellings, may be found at the back of the book. It is not exhaustive since to list all words, including those in the footnotes, would have been too cumbersome and quite impractical. But it should serve most readers well enough.

To the authors and all who contributed to *Building China* I owe my thanks. Their combined attempt to describe China's progress in terms of integrated development is a pioneering one which opens a new field of inquiry. I am especially indebted to the Social Welfare and Development Centre for Asia and the Pacific, a U. N. member agency in Manila, for its subsidy towards publication. Its Director, Dr. Ahmad Fattahipour, supported the project from beginning to end, ably assisted by SWDCAP's social welfare expert, Dr. J.F.X. Paiva. Where the contributors have drawn on research supported by particular grants, they footnote their acknowledgments individually, but I wish to add my voice in thanking each and every organization that lent a hand. Many individuals have been very helpful. Dr. Peter Acierto and Dr. Nelson W. S. Chow read the manuscript and offered their advice. Dr. John J. Deeney and Mrs. Li Wong Har-bing helped with the glossary. Mrs. Margaret Yaw deserves most credit for typing, since the bulk of it was done by her. My last, best word of thanks is for my wife, Lois, who proof-read everything.

JOHN F. JONES
The Chinese University of Hong Kong

CHAPTER ONE

China's Search for Integrated Development: An Overview

John F. Jones and John P. Burns

Economic, political, and social change has taken many forms in the People's Republic of China since 1949. In the countryside the ownership of land was gradually collectivized, land holdings rationalized, and agriculture put under central control. In the cities commerce and industry were taken over either by the state or by cooperatives. With these changes came a transition in the exercise and locus of power in Chinese society. The old gentry and landed classes of traditional China were replaced during the 1949 Land Reform by a new generation of political activists and Chinese Communist Party (CCP) members at various levels—mostly poor and middle peasants in rural areas, and in the cities intellectuals and workers. The class composition of the Chinese leadership changed radically.

These alterations in the economic and political spheres were accompanied by new policies in the social sphere. Class labels were given to people during Land Reform, a move which greatly affected their life chances after that. Ties to kinship and lineage associations, so powerful in rural areas, were weakened. Women were given property rights in an effort to make them full and equal partners in building China. Mass education was popularized.

These changes can all be seen as part of a unified approach to development, although the extent to which the process was truly integrated must be verified. This chapter will attempt a survey, a broad sweep of China's development since 1949, paying particular attention to its integration. Drawing on secondary and some primary material—party and government documents, press accounts in Chinese and in English translations, trip reports, and the like—we will examine chronologically the policies of the leadership in the economic, political, and social realms. And since plans are one thing and practice another, we will also take a look at the implementation of policies and popular reactions to them.

Post-liberation Chinese history can be divided into several periods: 1949-52, a time of consolidation; 1953-57, collectivization; 1958-59, the Great

Leap Forward; 1960-65, a period of recovery; 1966-69, the Cultural Revolution; and 1970-76, the post-Cultural Revolution years. During all of these periods there were economic, political, and social changes in China—without, as shall be seen, uniform progress on all fronts. We will attempt to examine each period in turn so that we may arrive at some general understanding of China's achievement during the past three decades.

CONSOLIDATION, 1949-52

By October 1, 1949, when Mao Tse-tung declared the establishment of the new People's Republic of China, fundamental changes in the economic and social structure were well under way in the "old base areas" of the Northwest. The agrarian reform, begun in many parts during the years 1937 to 1942, had called for the reduction of rents and cancellation of debts, foreshadowing the redistribution of land from landlords and rich peasants to poor peasants and hired laborers which was to come. In 1949 the right to land ownership of individual and corporate landlords was finally withdrawn throughout China, a move which signalled the most radical phase of the land revolution.[1]

As the People's Liberation Army (PLA) had gained control of the Yangtze River area and the southern provinces, land reform followed in its wake. Work teams composed of cadres from higher levels—usually party members and soldiers—fanned out throughout the countryside to implement the new agrarian policy. Associations of poor peasants were set up by the work teams to assign class labels to the rural population and then to distribute landlord property (the "fruits") among poor peasants and hired laborers. Class labels (landlord; rich, middle, and poor peasant; hired laborer) were assigned by the work teams and peasant associations in meetings lasting several days. Class designations depended on a family's property holdings, whether it had hired labor, and whether its members had worked in the fields themselves during the three years prior to Land Reform.[2]

The assigning of class labels came to affect the life chances of China's population during the following decades. Until quite recently, it was standard practice and approved policy in China to assign jobs, permit higher education, grant party membership, allow marriages, and give political rights on the basis

[1] "Basic Program on Chinese Agrarian Law," October 10, 1941, in Mark Selden (ed.), *The People's Republic of China: A Documentary History of Revolutionary Change* (New York: Monthly Review Press, 1979), p. 215.

[2] For an idea of the complexity of the task of class labelling, and indeed its contentiousness, see William Hinton, *Fanshen: A Documentary of Revolution in a Chinese Village* (New York: Vintage Books, 1966), pp. 297-300.

of these Land Reform class designations.[3] Their importance in determining the future life chances of the average Chinese cannot be over-emphasized.

In 1949 class labels were apportioned to the population roughly as follows:[4]

	Percentage of population
landlords	2.6
rich peasants	3.6
middle peasants	35.8
poor peasants and hired laborers	57.1

During Land Reform, landlords were put under supervision, and landlord properties distributed among poor peasants and hired laborers. Between 1949 and 1952, about 45 per cent of the farm land was redistributed to around 60 to 70 per cent of peasant households.[5] Of the land that changed ownership, two-thirds came from landlords, and less than one-third from rich peasants. Less than two-thirds of the land that changed hands went to poor peasants, while over one-third went to middle peasants.[6] Thus, while poor peasants gained much more land than they had rented previously, rich peasants still ended up with almost twice as much land as their poor peasant neighbors—a result in keeping with the comparatively moderate agrarian reform policy of 1950.[7]

Although production increased after Land Reform, in large measure because of the stability and the end to civil war which these policies heralded, the significance of the "land to the tiller" policy program went beyond productive output. It broke the local power structure which had been based on individual and corporate land ownership. Landlords were deprived of control of the land, the ability to rent property or to hire labor—deprived, in brief, of the instruments of power. Kinship and religious associations, whose power also rested on land ownership, were seriously undermined for they, too, could no longer own land, collect rents or hire labor.

[3] See "Mobilizing All Positive Factors," *Peking Review*, No. 7 (February 16, 1979), pp. 4-5, which indicates that the policy of discriminating against "bad classes" is changing in China. The change dates from late 1978.

[4] Peter Schran, *The Development of Chinese Agriculture, 1950-59* (Urbana, Ill.: University of Illinois Press, 1969), p. 21.

[5] Alexander Eckstein, *China's Economic Revolution* (Cambridge: Cambridge University Press, 1977), p. 68; and Schran, *op. cit.*, pp. 20-23.

[6] Schran, *op. cit.*, p. 23.

[7] "Report on the Question of Agrarian Reform," June 14, 1950. In Selden, *op. cit.*, pp. 238-239.

In place of the old system, new institutions were created by the CCP through the work teams. Political activists from poor and middle peasant backgrounds were cultivated for party membership and local leadership positions. The locus of power in the countryside shifted to the peasant associations, dominated by poor and middle peasant activists.

Rural society was also changed by the promulgation of the new Marriage Law in 1950.[8] It outlawed the "feudal" practice of arranged marriages, provided that men and women "enjoyed equal status within the home," gave women equal rights over property (including the right to inherit property), and acknowledged the right of both men and women to divorce. The thrust of the law was to undermine the superior position of men in Chinese society, for they alone had owned property, and decided questions of marriage and divorce in pre-1949 China. The law did not, however, end the practice of patrilocal marriages. Women continued to marry *in* to their husbands' families, deriving their status in the local community from their husband's family, a situation made worse by the rural practice of marrying outside the village. The women, therefore, were usually strangers in their husbands' village. Although women were recruited into leadership positions, their numbers were far fewer than males. Patrilocal marriage patterns were further reinforced by the practice of inheriting class labels through the male line. A son of a landlord retained his father's "bad class label," while a daughter of a landlord could marry a poor peasant, and produce poor peasant offspring. How rigidly the class system was enforced has varied since 1949. Throughout the years its importance was much more evident in rural areas than in the cities.[9]

The party consolidated its hold on the cities from 1949 to 1952 by taking a number of measures to gain at least indirect control of the economy.[10] Although large schools and factories owned by the Kuomintang (KMT) and foreigners were taken over directly, CCP urban policy called for gaining control of key industries and commodities as a way of guiding the economy. Organizational controls were the most important tool, coupled with a massive effort to collect demographic and production data. Census results enabled local governments to organize urban households into neighborhood groups. Industrial enterprises were registered, and contracts were signed with them on a selective basis for production of goods with state supplied raw materials at fixed prices. Commercial ventures, including hawkers, were also registered. Sites were allocated for commercial activities, and some commercial outlets

[8] "The Marriage Law of the PRC," April 13, 1950. In Selden, *op. cit.*, pp. 193-200.

[9] Richard Kraus, "Class Conflict and the Vocabulary of Social Analysis in China," *China Quarterly*, No. 69 (March 1977), pp. 54-74.

[10] This discussion is based on Ezra Vogel, *Canton under Communism: Programs and Politics in a Provincial Capital, 1949-1968* (New York: Harper and Row, 1969), pp. 71-77.

were selected as government agents for the sale of goods. During this early period, then, the government moved gradually to circumscribe the field of operations of commercial and industrial activity without actually taking direct control.

In addition to these measures, government increased taxation, set prices, controlled the availability of raw materials, and sold bonds to sometimes reluctant buyers, all in an effort to stabilize the economy under its control.

The mechanisms for enforcing compliance to the state were primarily political. Party committees were set up to guide factory managers and businessmen, but in addition mass organizations of political activists played a key role. Trade unions, for example, were charged with supervising factory pricing policies and the use of raw materials.

Two national campaigns aimed at bringing the bureaucracy and private business worlds into compliance were launched in 1952. The "Three Anti-" Campaign sought to reduce graft, waste, and bureaucratism in the public service, a consequence in part of the shortage of experienced cadres. The "Five Anti-" Campaign took businessmen as its target, and sought to root out bribery, tax evasion, expropriation of public property, cheating on government contracts, and stealing secret government economic data.

The period, 1949-52, was one of consolidation during which the CCP attempted to stabilize and gain control of the rural and urban economy and social institutions, while at the same time ensuring the continuation of production, distribution, and essential social services. The next period saw the first attempts to transform the economy and society—that is, to build socialism.

COLLECTIVIZATION, 1953-57

1953-57, the years marking the First Five-year Plan,[11] were heavily influenced by models inspired by the Soviet Union. The period was also characterized, according to Vogel, by something of a naive "faith in the power of statistics, science, and planning, matched by faith in the virtues of specialization."[12]

The economic plan placed most emphasis on achieving early industrialization, and, virtually ignoring agriculture, sought to concentrate state resources on the rapid development of heavy industry. Giant factories, mines, and engineering projects, almost all located in or near large cities, were given priority. Fifty eight per cent of the 42 billion *yuan* allocated for the plan was to go to industry, while only 7 per cent was allocated to agriculture.[13]

[11] This Plan was not promulgated, however, until 1955.

[12] Vogel, *op. cit.*, p. 127.

[13] Jean Chesneaux, *China: The People's Republic, 1949-76* (New York: Pantheon, 1979), p. 58.

Soviet influence predominated not only in the priorities chosen by the Chinese planners, but in the implementation of plans as well. By 1956, there were 10,000 Soviet experts in China advising in various capacities.[14]

However, several significant changes in rural organization, which cannot be traced to Soviet influence, were also in evidence during this period. By 1952-53, many areas had set up either seasonal or more permanent "mutual aid teams" to rationalize rural labor requirements. Six or more households pooled their labor and tools to cultivate individually-owned tracts of land. By 1954, some 58.3 per cent of households had been incorporated into these organizations.[15]

In 1954 the first lower stage agricultural producers' co-operatives (LAPC's) were formed in the countryside. Peasants pooled their land, labor and tools (i.e., invested them in the co-ops), and received profits based on the amount of the investment as well as their labor contribution. Co-op membership grew slowly in 1954, then more quickly in 1955 to incorporate 14.2 per cent of rural households. Thus, by 1955, 35 per cent of all rural households were farming individually, 51 per cent were members of mutual aid teams, and the remainder had joined co-ops.[16]

The "unified purchase and sale of grain," entailing output quotas for households and collectives, was introduced by the government in 1955. Production quotas were given to collective units and individuals alike, which sparked some resistance. Some units and individuals refused to supply necessary production data or under-reported output in the hope that quotas would be lowered. Others simply sold grain on the open market, refusing to comply with the state purchasing policy.[17]

During this time, some leaders in Peking and in the provinces sought to reduce the speed of collectivization.[18] Vice-Premier Teng Tzu-hui, an advocate of more gradual collectivization, preferred to wait until the material conditions in the countryside had improved. In 1955, reflecting this leadership dissension, peasants began withdrawing from co-ops, and some 200,000 were disbanded.[19] Dissatisfied with the slow pace, Mao went over the heads of his

[14] *Ibid.*, p. 58.

[15] Schran, *op. cit.*, p. 27.

[16] *Ibid.*, p. 28.

[17] See Thomas P. Bernstein, "Cadre and Peasant Behavior under Conditions of Insecurity and Deprivation: The Grain Supply Crisis of the Spring of 1955," in A. Doak Barnett (ed.), *Chinese Communist Policies in Action* (Seattle: University of Washington Press, 1969), pp. 365-400.

[18] See the March 1955 State Council Directive, "Directive on Spring Farming and Production," quoted in Paris Chang, *Power and Policy in China* (University Park, Pa.: Pennsylvania State University Press, 1975), p. 10.

[19] Chang, *op. cit.*, pp. 12-13.

opponents in the central government, and appealed directly to provincial level leaders for a speed-up of collectivization.

The result was the formation of higher-stage agricultural producers' co-operatives (HAPC's) in which peasants were remunerated *only* according to their labor contribution. Dividends were not paid for animals, tools, or land turned over to the HAPC's. Peasant households did, however, retain private plots (up to 5 per cent of the total cultivated area) and could sell their own produce at rural markets.

Official figures indicate that peasant households were organized into HAPC's very rapidly. By 1957, peasants farming individually comprised only 2 per cent of the population, all others being organized into higher-stage co-ops.[20] These figures conceal the fact that there was considerable local opposition at this stage of collectivization. Livestock and pig populations, for example, decreased dramatically in some areas, as peasants sought to consume them rather than see them collectivized.[21] In other areas, some peasants sought to withdraw from the co-ops as soon as pressure from above was relaxed.

Transformation of the urban economy kept pace with these changes in rural areas, so that by mid-1955, just as agricultural co-operativization reached its peak, collectivization of commerce and industry was well advanced. Large businesses were put under state control as joint state-private ventures, often retaining their former owners as managers. Small commercial enterprises and industrial concerns were organized into co-operatives. The government also moved to make retailers into government agents for foods it controlled, and then took over direct control of most wholesaling. By late 1955 in Canton, for example, only 54 per cent of output was in private hands, compared to 87 per cent in 1952. And by January 1956, socialist transformation in the cities (as in the rural areas) was speeded up, so that by late 1957, 99.4 per cent of the value of industrial output and 95.7 per cent of trade turnover was under state, joint public-private, or co-operative ownership in this one large representative city.[22]

These changes did not go unopposed. Prior to being taken over, some businessmen withdrew capital from their businesses, or shut them down altogether. But resistance was very mild compared to opposition in the countryside.

The government sought to dampen resistance by organizing friendly businessmen to act as mediators. In Canton, for example, the Federation of Industry and Commerce, organized by well-known capitalists willing to cooperate with the government, served this function.[23] Supervision within

[20] Schran, *op. cit.*, p. 28.

[21] See Kenneth R. Walker, *Planning in Chinese Agriculture: Socialization and the Private Sector, 1956-62* (Chicago: Aldine, 1965).

[22] Vogel, *op. cit.*, p. 173.

[23] *Ibid.*, pp. 157, 161, 173.

commercial and industrial enterprises was concentrated in the hands of government and party cadres, while the technical questions of how to implement policies were left in the hands of enterprise managers.

Mao's reappraisal of divisions within post-Liberation Chinese society sought to explain this opposition to collectivization at the local and national level. In an important essay, "On the Correct Handling of Contradictions among the People," Mao recognized in socialist societies two different sources of opposition (or contradictions).[24] Opposition could come from within the people, such as conflict between peasants and workers. This he considered a non-antagonistic contradiction. Or it could come from opponents of the people, that is, the counter-revolutionaries. This latter was an antagonistic contradiction which separated counter-revolutionaries and class enemies from the people. The new analysis declared the opposition to collectivization in the countryside and the cities to be non-antagonistic because it came from within the people. But it also offered a novel and very radical interpretation of what constituted the basis of social class. Rather than tying class distinctions to property relations as Marx had done—and Mao himself had previously done —Mao declared that attitudes and behavior were key determinants of a person's class status. Counter-revolutionaries were those who thought or behaved in a counter-revolutionary manner regardless of their or their families' property ownership in the past. This analysis gave new life to the class struggle in China. Class contradictions, Mao was saying, would continue under socialism.

The analysis helped to explain not only local opposition, but opposition from within the leadership itself. In 1954, for example, Kao Kang, head of the Organization Department of the Central Committee and an important figure in Manchuria, was dismissed as a "hidden counter-revolutionary" who had tried to seize power. Throughout the period, opposition to more rapid collectivization kept resurfacing in Peking. But it was only in May 1956 that the extent of elite opposition became obvious, and it shocked the leadership. Secure in the knowledge that collectivization was progressing and production increasing, the leadership had sought to strengthen its relationship with intellectuals, a group whose support it needed to develop the economy, under the slogan "Let a hundred flowers bloom, let a hundred schools of thought contend." After some hesitation, a torrent of criticism poured forth from writers, editors, scientists, teachers, and other professionals—demanding in some cases more freedom from party control, and even questioning the justification for the party's monopoly of state power. A severe anti-rightist campaign in 1957 and the labeling of thousands of intellectuals, cadres, and businessmen

[24] Mao Tse-tung, "On the Correct Handling of Contradictions among the People" (February 27, 1957), in *Selected Works of Mao Tse-tung* (Peking: Foreign Languages Press), Vol. 5, pp. 384-421.

as "rightists" ended the outburst. They became members of the "five bad elements"—counter-revolutionaries, rightists, landlords, rich peasants, and criminals—to be officially discriminated against as "outside" the people.[25]

The period 1953-57 was one of rapid economic growth and great organizational changes in the economy. It also saw experimentation in the regime's relations with its most powerful potential critics, the intellectuals. Mao's clamping down on dissent in 1957 served as a prelude to the campaign which was to follow.

THE GREAT LEAP FORWARD, 1958-59

As early as 1956 Chinese leaders expressed doubts about the utility of the Soviet model for developing industry and education. Giving priority to heavy industry while ignoring small-scale production and agriculture had jeopardized long-term industrialization. They came to see that only a more productive and efficient agricultural establishment could finance industrialization. By 1957, gains in agriculture were declining, a development that had to be changed. Mao's solution was yet another reorganization.

The "Great Leap Forward," as the 1958 campaign came to be known, was characterized by administrative decentralization, sending down cadres to local units to implement state policy, construction of small-scale urban and rural industrial projects, and a massive mobilization of labor on construction projects.

The campaign is best seen within the international and national environment of the time. Relations with the Soviet Union were strained, not only because of Khrushchev's denunciation of Stalin in 1956, but also because Soviet solutions to Chinese development problems were coming to be seen as inadequate. The KMT on Taiwan were making belligerent noises, and an American-backed military operation may have been seen as a real possibility by Peking. The Korean War was still a fresh memory. All of these signs pointed to the need to develop quickly and to become much more self-reliant.

To problematic external circumstances must be added the doubts of some leaders in Peking. Agricultural problems were seen as holding back industrial growth. China's greatest resource, labor, must then be reorganized to boost agriculture. Although the Second Five-Year Plan continued to emphasize heavy industry, for the first time it acknowledged the importance of agriculture in the slogan "walking on two legs." Politically, after the shock of the

[25]This group was more recently been rehabilitated. Teng Hsiao-p'ing sought the services of a wide variety of experts, professionals and the like in the "Four Modernizations" drive. Thousands of those labeled "rightists" in 1957 had their labels changed in 1978-79.

"Hundred Flowers" criticisms, the regime may have seen a need for dramatic results, a need which Mao felt could be served by demonstrating the superiority of a more radical reorganization of agricultural production.

In the countryside Mao called for the creation of people's communes— new administrative and production units that would integrate the functions of government, industry, commerce, and social welfare. Communes were established by amalgamating HAPC's, and varied in size from 20,000 to 80,000 people. By December 1958, authorities reported that 99 per cent of China's peasantry was organized into 26,578 communes. These, in turn, were subdivided into brigades, each further divided into ten or more production teams, a form of organization which continues to this day in the countryside. The commune in 1958 was taken to be the accounting unit—profits and wages were figured on a commune-wide basis.

Several changes were made in the incentive system which affected peasant households. Peasants were no longer permitted to retain private plots, rural markets were discontinued, household sideline industries for family profit were prohibited, and peasants were encouraged to eat with several hundred others in communal dining halls. Efforts were made to increase the labor contribution of women and students. Women, burdened with the care of their children, cooking meals, and other domestic duties, had previously been less able to participate in field work as a result. The Great Leap Forward sought to change this by establishing child care facilities and assuming responsibility for meals. The mobilization of labor was perhaps the most significant feature of the period.

In many parts these changes were accompanied by a new distribution system based on need rather than labor contribution. Called the "free supply system," it divorced payments to commune members from labor contribution or productivity. Experimenting with this system lasted only briefly, since not a few areas faced food shortages as early as 1959.

In urban areas, communal reorganization was tried briefly from 1958 to 1960. These arrangements sought to link urban areas with nearby rural areas under a common administration. This reorganization was designed to ease the flow of agricultural products to the cities, thus to increase food supplies. The urban commune organization integrated governmental, social welfare, and industrial-commercial activities, just as did the rural people's communes. Urban areas sought to draw on new labor resources—housewives and students —for work on construction projects. Small neighborhood workshops and industries were also established to tap this previously unused or under-used labor supply. Communal dining halls and day-care centers were organized briefly as a part of this campaign.

In both urban and rural areas the Great Leap Forward was characterized by decentralization of power and authority. Peking retained control over output targets, but permitted a great deal of local initiative as to how these quotas might be met. Up to 20 per cent of profits in industry could be retained locally under the new measures, local adjustments of budgets were permitted, and reporting was simplified. Bureaucrats were moved from national and provincial levels to county levels, and enterprises themselves were put under local control.[26] From 1957 to 1959 the percentage of industries under central control fell from 46 to 26 per cent.[27]

These changes in the distribution of power in urban and rural areas, and the policies of the Great Leap Forward itself had an enormous impact on China's development. In the economic realm, China experienced a serious depression from 1959 to 1961 ("the three bad years") which required another four years for production again to reach 1957 levels.[28] The causes of the economic crisis were many, not the least of which was bad weather affecting the harvests during those years. But several man-made causes were just as important: (1) The complete collapse of the reporting system, under pressure from Peking to produce results commensurate with wildly inflated quotas, resulted in the temporary suspension of realistic planning in China for several years. (Peking initially lost some measure of control of the planning-reporting system as early as 1957 when measures to decentralize were initiated).[29] (2) The mobilization of labor on ambitious capital construction projects resulted in a shortage of rural laborers and meant that agricultural work was often left undone. This, in conjunction with bad weather, affected food output.[30] (3) Many construction projects, often hastily conceived and sometimes badly designed, had to be abandoned only partially completed when flooding occurred. This made the effects of the natural disasters even worse.

The political consequences, in some ways less obvious, were just as severe. In order to meet inflated quotas, local cadres resorted to authoritarian tactics ("commandism"), and, in desperation, submitted false reports which exaggerated output. The decentralization of power, while intended to leave managers and commune heads with more room to maneuver, also allowed local party committees to take the initiative. They came to dominate even the most technical functions of enterprise and commune management.

In the social realm the Great Leap Forward had a major impact. Setting up

[26]Vogel, op. cit., pp. 224-225.

[27]Chesneaux, op. cit., p. 94.

[28]Ibid., p. 100.

[29]See Li Choh-ming, The Statistical System of Communist China (Berkeley: University of California Press, 1962).

[30]Leslie T. C. Kuo, The Technical Transformation of Agriculture in Communist China (New York: Praeger, 1972), pp. 88-92.

communes in the countryside permitted a commune-wide solution to welfare problems. During this period changes were made in education policy in an attempt to undercut the impact of family socialization. Boarding nurseries and primary schools were experimented with during the more radical phase of the campaign. While some of the new education policies faded away with time, others lasted, particularly the policy of tying education directly to production. Part-work, part-study education—a product of the Great Leap Forward—was seen as a way to make education more practical and meet increasing demands for labor. Schools established relationships with workshops, and students and teachers worked on construction sites.[31]

But the decentralization measures of the Great Leap Forward resulted in a tendency toward disintegration of the national economic planning system. The center, while retaining control of paper targets, lost its ability to plan effectively. Local units, feigning compliance by submitting false and exaggerated reports, further undermined the planning system. As Vogel put it, "The dispersion of power, like the original centralization of power, was overdone; central ministries were no longer given the information and power they needed to coordinate the national economy."[32]

On the national level, when it became obvious that Mao's initiatives had failed, opposition to the Leap grew within the leadership. Mao resigned as Head of State in 1958 (the post went to Liu Shao-ch'i), and assumed, at least verbally, responsibility for the failure.[33] Criticism of the campaign mounted and was symbolized by the confrontation between Mao and Defense Minister Peng Teh-huai at the Lushan Plenum in 1959. Peng was dismissed for his opposition. This split within the leadership was later to grow into the open confrontation of the Cultural Revolution.

RECOVERY, 1960-65

By 1960 the radical initiatives of Mao's Great Leap Forward were in decline and a more moderate policy was being advocated by planners in Peking. In 1960-62 agriculture was reorganized by increasing the number of communes, while reducing the size of each to more manageable proportions. The incentive system was restructured to reward individual households and small groups of cultivators. Private plots were restored, and household sideline activities and rural markets were encouraged. The "free supply system" was replaced by a modified piece-rate system that tied income to labor contributions. At the

[31]Chesneaux, op. cit., p. 91.
[32]Vogel, op. cit., p. 226.
[33]Stuart Schram, Chairman Mao Talks to the People (New York: Pantheon, 1975), pp. 142-145.

same time, first the brigade,[34] and then the production team (usually composed of 20 to 40 households) was made the unit of accounting, a move that caused difficulties for less well endowed teams and tended to increase, not reduce, income differentials in the countryside. It did, however, spur production by rewarding wealthier teams.[35] These policy changes were symbolized by the slogan, "three freedoms and one guarantee" (free extension of private plots, sideline production, and rural markets, and the fixing of output quotas for the household rather than the collective). The intention was to encourage peasant productivity.

The changes tended to strengthen the cohesiveness of teams and brigades, or natural villages, but to reduce horizontal integration among villages. A consequence of organizing rural units of production around (village) residential units was that peasants tended to identify their kinship group with the team or brigade, especially in single surname villages. This development was largely unanticipated by China's leaders, and contradicted policy of weakening kinship ties while strengthening class solidarity. Educational policies encouraging "self-sufficiency" in rural village schooling, marketing policies restricting the number of intermediate market towns, and marriage policies encouraging marriages within villages all worked to reduce horizontal integration, isolating villages from their surroundings.[36]

A number of problems began to emerge in the countryside. Lowering the accounting unit to the production team increased the opportunities for corruption among local cadres. Brigade and team cadres accepted bribes, embezzled funds, set prices, and expropriated work points. One confidential internal report disclosed that:

> In the Ch'ih-shih brigade, the brigade chief, accountant and cashier (all three of whom are party members) together with the party branch secretary as the leader, have engaged collectively in graft of public funds. From September 1961 to September 1962 they did not record income on the accounts. They falsified bank receipts, destroyed stubs, and appropriated cash under false names. They committed graft amounting to 1,394 *yuan*, involving misappropriation for sale of brigade cedar and bamboo and misappropriation of funds. In addition they borrowed 422.72 *yuan* of public funds.[37]

---

[34] "Urgent Directive Concerning Present Policy Problems in the Rural People's Communes," in Selden, *op. cit.*, p. 516.

[35] See the "Sixty Articles" in Union Research Institute, *Documents of Chinese Communist Party Central Committee, September 1956-April 1969* (Hong Kong: Union Research Institute, 1971), Vol. 1, pp. 695-725.

[36] William Parish, "China—Team, Brigade or Commune?" *Problems of Communism*, 25 March-April, 1976, pp. 51-56.

[37] C. S. Chen (ed.), *Rural People's Communes in Lien-Chiang* (Stanford: Stanford University Press, 1969), p. 196.

Associated with this disturbing development was the re-emergence of "feudal" and wasteful practices associated in the leadership's mind with the pre-Liberation period. Bride prices were being paid by the groom's family for marriage contracts, extravagant wedding and funeral banquets were being held even by cadres, gifts were exchanged at holidays, feasts were held to mark bumper crop harvests, pigs were privately slaughtered, and state property—whether land or timber—was being taken over for private use.[38] Reports of these deviations made their way to Peking, and prompted Mao to launch the Socialist Education Campaign in 1963, an attempt to change the thought and behavior of peasants and local cadres alike.

In urban areas, too, policy changes were initiated in an effort to restore production and alleviate food shortages. The incentive system in industry was established once again to reward productivity (with explicit wage grades reintroduced), but attention was also paid to improving accounting practices and specialist training. Efforts were made to raise the quality of goods produced, and the general retrenchment saw many of the small-scale industries closed down, as wasteful and inefficient.[39]

A significant feature of urban society during this period was the program to send youths to the countryside, which first reached a peak in 1964 (and again in 1968 during the Cultural Revolution). The purposes of the program were many. The program sought to reduce the differences between urban and rural areas by educating both populations in the ways of the other; it also sought to alleviate urban unemployment. The program came to be seen by many as a form of punishment for children with "bad" or only neutral class backgrounds. But it was resented by the peasant population, since rural communities were expected to feed, clothe, and house these youths, who, because of their urban upbringing, made only marginal contributions to rural production.

Some sent-down youth, however, were able to integrate into local rural communities. They married peasants, and took over leadership posts, particularly those jobs requiring literacy and accounting skills. And they aided the transfer of technology from urban research institutes by popularizing new agricultural techniques.[40]

Generally speaking, the economy recovered from the blow administered by the Great Leap Forward, and grew quickly after 1962. Grain production, which fell from 206 million metric tons in 1958 to 156 m.m.t. in 1960, rose to 194 m.m.t. by 1965.[41] The production of coal, crude oil, steel, and

[38]*Ibid.*, p. 197.   [39]Vogel, *op. cit.*, pp. 284-285.

[40]See Thomas Bernstein, *Up to the Mountain and Down to the Villages: The Transfer of Youth from Urban to Rural China* (New Haven: Yale University Press, 1977).

[41]Christopher Howe, *China's Economy: A Basic Guide* (New York: Basic Books, 1978), p. 72.

chemical fertilizer, all of which had fallen in 1960-61, grew quickly during these years, although coal output by 1964 was still less than in 1958-59.[42] The period, then, was one of rapid economic growth, and the aim was to recover the ground lost in 1958-59.

Social welfare policies, broadly defined, tended to serve the needs of the economy during this period, just as they had in previous years. Education was popularized, and by 1960-61, 85 per cent of the primary school population was attending school. Although the part-work, part-study schools set up in 1958-59 continued in rural areas, the renewed emphasis on specialization and increasing quality saw more resources poured into urban and higher education. In addition, in both urban and rural education, an officially sanctioned two-track system existed. Brighter students were encouraged to continue their education while the majority were channelled into technical careers. Model schools existed in each of these tracks. These model schools had better student-teacher ratios, large grants of state aid, and modern teaching materials. Admission to model schools was based on class background and achievement. The network of model (or "key point") schools extended throughout the country. Each province, district and county had model schools into which it poured disproportionately more resources. Students who graduated from these schools had a better chance of entering a university with the result that the college student population tended to come from urban and/or cadre backgrounds.[43]

Population planning was beginning to be taken seriously by 1961. Even in 1954, some leaders had advocated a population control policy, and in 1956-57 progress was reported in urban areas, but this was interrupted by the Great Leap Forward. By 1960-61, population control policies were again promoted, and by 1963 planned-birth commissions were established in each province. Local clinics and the women's federation were used in rural areas to propagate family planning. In rural Guangdong in 1965, according to one study, there was a growing awareness of birth control and its desirability, but these rural areas lacked the means to deliver contraceptives effectively or to mobilize peasants to use them.[44] One measure of the problem, however, was the fact that the Chinese government had not taken a census since 1953, and reliable population statistics simply did not exist.

[42]Chesneaux, *op. cit.*, p. 100.

[43]Suzanne Pepper, "Education and Revolution: The 'Chinese Model' Revised," *Asian Survey*, Vol. 18, No. 9 (September 1978), pp. 851-852.

[44]William Parish and Martin Whyte, *Village and Family in Contemporary China* (Chicago: University of Chicago Press, 1979), pp. 140-141. For an account of Shanghai's successful efforts to reduce population growth, see Lynn T. White III, *Careers in Shanghai* (Berkeley: University of California Press, 1978), pp. 200-206.

In the political arena, Mao, who had suffered a decline due to the failure of the Leap, sought to reassert his position by means of the Socialist Education Campaign, which was his response to reports of deviant behavior at local levels. He issued the "First Ten Points" in May 1963,[45] which called for "the cleaning up" of local cadres, establishing poor and lower-middle peasant associations, and the recording of local histories. This rather moderate document—emphasizing lenient treatment by education and persuasion of errant local cadres and peasants—was later seen as the opening salvo of the "Four Clean-Ups" Campaign (cleaning up accounts, granaries, work points, and collective property) which directly attacked local cadre corruption.

Implementation of the campaign was put in the hands of Teng Hsiao-p'ing, then Party Secretary-General, and Liu Shao-ch'i, Head of State, who issued two subsequent directives, the "Second Ten Points" in September 1963, and the "Revised Second Ten Points" a year later, which Mao subsequently claimed perverted the campaign and obstructed the true interests of the party. These policy statements took a much harsher line with local cadres, and resulted in the dismissal of large numbers of local rural leaders.

The Peking leadership sent work teams to the countryside to implement the Four Clean-Ups Campaign. The work team carried out their tasks zealously, with the result that between 1½ and 2 million cadres lost their posts. But the leadership seems not to have anticipated Mao's anger, and was unprepared when he issued his "Twenty-three Points" in January 1965. This directive called for moderation, and identified for the first time the source of the problem as "power holders within the party who are taking the capitalist road." The focus of conflict now shifted to the party bureaucracy in Peking and in the provinces. The stage was set for the Cultural Revolution.

THE CULTURAL REVOLUTION, 1966-69

The Cultural Revolution has been interpreted in many ways: as a power struggle among rival elite factions in Peking that spilled over into the provinces; as a policy dispute between two different groups with each advocating its own set of economic, political, and social priorities (a "two line struggle" between socialism and communism); as an attack on the excessive bureaucratism of post-revolutionary China; as an attempt to socialize millions of young people into a revolutionary struggle ethic which they were too young to have experienced previously; and as an attempt to purge Chinese culture

[45] For the Socialist Education Campaign documents, see Richard Baum and Frederick Teiwes, *Ssu-Ch'ing: The Socialist Education Movement of 1962-66* (Berkeley: University of California Press, 1968).

and education of bourgeois values. The Cultural Revolution was all of these.

The sequence of events in the Cultural Revolution is simple enough. By 1965 Mao saw that opposition to his policies was concentrated in the party and state bureaucracies at the highest levels. Liu Shao-ch'i, Teng Hsiao-p'ing, and other senior leaders distorted his policy initiatives in the process of implementation. From Mao's perspective, they as the party's leaders were putting themselves above party discipline. He therefore went outside the party and organized a force, the Red Guards, to attack the party establishment at national, provincial, district, and county levels. The attack prompted a counter-attack, with the office holders organizing their own Red Guard groups, a move that resulted in intense factionalism within the party, state, and urban organizations. Thousands of cadres at all levels were dismissed in the struggle that followed. A chaotic situation resulted in which factories ceased producing, schools were closed, and suburban agricultural production declined, as Red Guard factions fought it out among themselves. Only the army had sufficient national organizational capacity and discipline to bring the Red Guards into line. When the disturbances had reached a peak and were clearly out of hand, Mao called in the army to restore order. In 1969 the army, under the leadership of Lin Piao, suppressed the Red Guard factions, and set up new administrative organizations called revolutionary committees. These, at least in the countryside, were largely staffed by the pre-Cultural Revolution elite. The revolutionary committees in the rural areas were really the brigade and commune management committees under a different name.

The Cultural Revolution was primarily an urban campaign, with limited effects on the countryside. Struggles between various Red Guard factions, and attacks on commune and brigade party officials did spill over into some suburban areas. In 1967 informants from Guangdong, for example, reported a several months period of "no government" when local leaders, who had been attacked and suspended during the Four Clean-Ups Campaign in 1963-65, found themselves under attack again, and simply refused to carry out official duties.[46]

Policies associated with the Cultural Revolution, however, influenced rural life. Small-scale rural industrialization was once more fostered in a move to popularize self-reliance. Instead of the State investing resources in agriculture, each local unit was encouraged to pull itself up by its bootstraps (a policy which, incidentally, tended to widen income differentials between the better endowed and poorer production units.)

The incentive system was again re-structured, following the lead of the

[46] Richard Baum, "The Cultural Revolution in the Countryside: Anatomy of a Limited Rebellion," in Thomas W. Robinson (ed.), *The Cultural Revolution in China* (Berkeley: University of California Press, 1971), pp. 367-477.

national model brigade, Tachai, in Shansi province. Work points were to be distributed primarily according to one's political attitude and demonstrated political activism, and only secondarily according to one's labor contribution. In practice, political attitudes and activism had little influence on the distribution of income. Piece-rate distribution systems continued to be used in most places especially during the busy seasons, and during slack times a combination of piece-rate and time-rate was common.

Health care co-operatives were also set up in response to Cultural Revolution policy initiatives. Modest monthly contributions entitled participating families to free medical care in brigade clinics and commune-run hospitals. Barefoot doctors, trained and equiped to treat minor ailments and to act as midwives, extended paramedical services to rural areas. Coupled with this program was one which provided basic social security for the elderly—the "Five Guarantees," assuring each team member food, shelter, clothing, medical care, and burial expenses. Originally designed to guarantee peasant security in the 1950s, the program was re-emphasized during the Cultural Revolution but, as Parish and Whyte point out, ". . . these guarantees were to apply only to old people who had no grown sons to support them. . . ."[47] Social welfare was, therefore, a local matter, chiefly supplied by rural households themselves. Indeed, Parish and Whyte found that only a small number of team members (averaging 1.24 persons per team) in the Guangdong villages about which they had information received any public support.

The Cultural Revolution affected rural education. Primary schooling—both urban and rural—was cut from six to five years, and the duration of both lower and upper middle schools was reduced from three to two years. Funding for rural education continued to come from local resources. Cultural Revolution reforms were designed to reduce educational differences not only within and between villages, but also between rural and urban areas, a result achieved by establishing brigade-run middle schools. Parish and Whyte note that in the villages they surveyed in Guangdong "there were almost no brigade-run lower middle schools" before the Cultural Revolution; but by 1973, three fourths of the brigades surveyed had them. They conclude that in rural areas the outer forms of Cultural Revolution reforms in education had been largely complied with in the years between 1968 and 1973.[48]

If the disruption to rural areas was relatively limited, the same cannot be said for the cities. Red Guard groups were well organized and permeated every production and/or residential unit in most urban areas.[49] The legacy

[47] Parish and Whyte, *op. cit.*, p. 75.
[48] *Ibid.*, p. 81.
[49] See Neale Hunter, *Shanghai Journal: An Eyewitness Account of the Cultural Revolution* (Boston: Beacon Press, 1969).

of the attacks on office holders which came to characterize the Cultural Revolution has been one of intense factionalism, especially in the major centers like Shanghai, Wuhan, Canton, Kueichow, and Chengtu.

Cultural Revolution policies greatly influenced life in urban areas. Most large cities, for example, put all urban housing, a large amount of which had been privately owned until that time, under municipal control.[50] Changes in urban incentive policies mirrored rural changes in their emphasis on political attitudes and behavior. The industrial incentive policies of the 1960s (especially piece-rates, bonuses, and wage increases) were harshly criticized, and emphasis was placed on normative and group material incentives.[51] Factory managers who had advocated that production be related to profits, that profits be retained in the enterprise, and that specialists and technicians be employed to increase the quality of production, were denounced for putting "profits in command."

Demands for worker participation in decisions, which during the 1960s had been the prerogative of managers, were raised by some urban Red Guard groups.[52] Committees of workers at sub-factory level were to be given more power, and workers were to be consulted on major decisions. But how far these policies were ever implemented is unknown.[53]

These policy changes, championed by that segment of the leadership closely associated with Mao, were accompanied by a radical critique of China's education system. Education, Mao said, was too heavily examination oriented; it favored children of intellectual and "bourgeois" backgrounds; it did not value production or manual labor; and it failed to serve the needs of China's workers and peasants. Mao's own views are best stated by himself:

> At present, there is too much studying going on, and this is exceedingly harmful. There are too many subjects at present, and the burden is too heavy.... The syllabus should be chopped in half.... Our present method of conducting examinations is a method for dealing with the enemy, not a method for dealing with the people. It is a method of surprise attack, asking oblique or strange questions....
> I am in favor of publishing the questions in advance and letting the students study

---

[50]Much of this housing was returned to private owners in subsequent years. Housing has always been privately owned in the countryside, except in a few model units.

[51]See Carl Riskin, "Maoism and Motivation: Work Incentives in China," *Bulletin of Concerned Asian Scholars*, July 1973, pp. 10-35, where the case is made that China has always emphasized some kind of material incentives but that the emphasis has shifted back and forth between *group* material incentives and *individual* material incentives.

[52]"Hold High the Great Red Banner of the Thought of Mao Tse-tung, Further Deepen the Revolutionization of Enterprises: Basic Experience of Revolutionization of the Tach'ing Oil Field," in Selden, *op. cit.*, pp. 584-585.

[53]For a contrasting opinion of events, see Steve Andors, *China's Industrial Revolution: Politics, Planning and Management* (New York: Pantheon, 1977).

them and answer them with the aid of books. . . . At examinations, whispering
into each other's ears and taking other people's places ought to be allowed. If
your answer is good and I copy it, then mine should be counted as good.[54]

These views gained the upper hand during the Cultural Revolution, and in
1967-68 schools were shut down altogether. Text books were rewritten, and
teachers reeducated. "Going against the tide," questioning and challenging
educational authority, was encouraged.

When schools re-opened in 1969 the new education policy reflected these
criticisms. Entrance examinations to primary, secondary, and higher educational institutions were abolished. They were replaced by a system of recommendations by production leaders and teachers. The purpose was to benefit
children of poor and lower-middle peasants and workers. Class origins were
stressed, and only children from good class backgrounds could gain admission
to senior middle schools or graduate institutions. Emphasis was put on expanding enrollments to reduce the inequalities of the 1960s' educational
system. Course curricula were revised so that 60 to 70 per cent of class time
could be devoted to general knowledge and productive labor courses, with 30
to 40 per cent devoted to politics. Committees replaced school heads, and
workers and peasants were expected to take part in school management.[55]

New forms of part-time education were experimented with. They included
short training courses, correspondence courses, factory-run universities, farm
universities, and hospital-run medical schools.[56]

Taken as a whole, the Cultural Revolution had its greatest impact on
education, the economy and, of course, on politics. Towards the end of the
period, 1969-70, universal primary education began to make great strides.
Many of the educational reforms continued past 1970 and were implemented
in the ensuing years. The program which sent large numbers of educated youth
to the countryside was expanded during the Cultural Revolution, reaching its
peak in 1968.[57] Those youths permitted to remain in the cities—the children
of influential cadres and of parents with good class backgrounds (and without
"political problems")—were assigned urban jobs by the Municipal Labor
Bureaus.

If the Cultural Revolution countered pressure to increase wages, it had
other negative affects on the economy. Although industrial and agricultural

[54]Stuart Schram, *Mao Tse-tung Unrehearsed* (Harmondsworth: Penguin Books,
1974), pp. 197-211.
[55]Pepper, *op. cit.*, pp. 852-856.
[56]"The Road for Training Engineering and Technical Personnel Indicated by the
Shanghai Machine Tools Plant," in Selden, *op. cit.*, pp. 602-606.
[57]It has been estimated that 13.2 million youths were sent to the countryside from
1958-75. Bernstein, *Up to the Mountains*, p. 2.

output continued to grow during the Cultural Revolution, the rate of growth from 1965 to 1970 was sharply reduced, and actually fell in 1968-69, the result chiefly of turmoil in the factories (some were shut down completely, others suspended work), the interruption of transportation services and especially the railroads, breakdowns in the supply of raw materials, and paralysis in rural state purchasing departments.[58]

The end of the period saw political power at local levels in the countryside returned to the pre-Cultural Revolution elite in the majority of places. Where the Cultural Revolution activists gained most was in urban areas, and within the party leaderships at higher levels, positions they were able to maintain until 1976. Many of the old national leaders—including Liu Shao-ch'i, Teng Hsiao-p'ing and their supporters—were in disgrace. The army, at the request of Mao himself, had stepped in to restore order, and there was a semblance of unity.

THE STRUGGLE CONTINUED, 1970-76

Cultural Revolution policies dominated education and industry from 1970 to 1976. In agriculture, however, after a brief experiment with the more radical policies of the Cultural Revolution from 1969 to 1971, these agricultural policies were abruptly discontinued in 1971, coinciding with the purge of Lin Piao. In 1973, at Chou En-lai's insistence, Teng Hsiao-p'ing was returned to power, and this signalled a renewed struggle over the future course of China's development priorities. A campaign was launched in 1975 by Chiang Ch'ing and her supporters (all victors in the Cultural Revolution) to oust Teng for his alleged "reversal of Cultural Revolution verdicts," and for encouraging a "rightist wind." The T'ien-an-men riots in April 1976 provided a convenient pretext, and Teng was sacked yet again in the same decision that unexpectedly elevated Hua Kuo-feng to the Chairmanship of the Party.

This political instability had little impact on local rural development, however. Rural organizational structure has remained relatively stable since the 1962 reforms. From 1969 to 1971 there was pressure on local leaders to adopt a series of radical measures. Higher levels called for the amalgamation of production teams (thereby effectively expanding the unit of accounting), the taking over of team sideline enterprises, the restricting of private plots and family sideline activities. The leadership also permitted and advocated the use of team labor forces for capital construction projects. There was once again emphasis on group incentives. Changes along these lines were implemented in

[58] Howe, *op. cit.*, p. xxiii.

many places. By 1971, however, it was clear that they were hampering productivity, and they were scrapped.[59] The next few years saw official denunciations of the leftist excesses of this short period.

In subsequent years, rural China was mobilized in a campaign to build Tachai-type counties, but the movement came to mean emulation of Tachai's spirit of self-reliance rather than copying Tachai's example of restricting private plots and private housing. The campaign sought to modernize China's agricultural sector. Electrification, mechanization, and increased fertilizer output were its chief objectives. By 1975, 70 per cent of communes had their own electricity supply, coming mainly from 60,000 small hydro-electric stations scattered around the country. Most of the rural electricity supply, in fact, had been used to drive irrigation equipment. To maximize use of this new energy source, therefore, agricultural policy attempted to popularize the use of pumps and other smaller equipment. Tractors were also introduced on a wide scale, so that during this period no less than 10 per cent of cultivated land was worked by tractors. Output was also increased in the 1970s by increasing the production and distribution of chemical fertilizers to supplement night soil, used in most areas. Indeed, fertilizer output grew by at least 17 per cent per annum during the 1960s and 1970s. From a total supply of 0.39 million metric tons in 1952, Chinese farmers were able to draw on 30.98 m.m.t. in 1975.[60]

Serious attempts to introduce a birth control policy in rural areas were made during these years. The target was to reduce natural population increases in the countryside to 15 per 1,000. In some areas, the authorities established strong disincentives for having more children. The fourth child in many production teams received no regular grain, cotton, sugar, oil, or fish rations. Private plots, extended for the first few children, were not extended for the fourth child. More birth control devices became available during the period, and sterilizations and abortions were provided free of charge. Parish and Whyte conclude that in Guangdong, for example, the planned births policy appeared to have had considerable success.[61]

---

[59]"CCP Central Committee Directive Concerning the Question of Distribution in Rural People's Communes," 26 December, 1971, in *Issues and Studies*, November 1972, pp. 92-95.

[60]Howe, *op. cit.*, pp. 87-90.

[61]Parish and Whyte, *op. cit.*, pp. 141-154. Note that during the Great Leap Forward and again during the Cultural Revolution birth control was no longer official policy. During these periods the benefits of population increases (more labor in a labor intensive economy) were emphasized, and the voices calling for a planned births policy were publicly ridiculed. The economic rationale for a planned births policy is illustrated in Arthur G. Ashbrook, Jr., "China: Economic Overview, 1975," in Joint Economic Committee, *China: A Reassessment of the Economy* (Washington, D.C.: Government Printing Office, 1975), p. 25.

Urban areas continued to experiment with Cultural Revolution policies in education, commerce, and industry until 1976. The changes in education, enumerated above, were implemented with considerable variation throughout China during these years. The guidelines for shortening primary and middle schooling were carried out in some areas (e.g., Peking), but not in others (e.g., Shanghai and Shenyang).[62] Teaching materials were gradually standardized on a provincial basis, in some cases as early as 1970, but in other cases much later. But grades and academic achievement were emphasized. Students continued to receive practical training and to be sent to the countryside.[63]

Higher education continued to be affected by the Cultural Revolution policies. Admissions were based on recommendations, not examinations, a policy which benefited less well qualified rural youths, and class background continued to be crucial. Children of the "five bad elements" or urban capitalists and intellectuals could not usually advance beyond junior middle school. Curricula reflected Cultural Revolution policies. Textbooks and course materials at university level were re-written gradually, and libraries reopened, minus the "poisonous weeds" of the 1960s. The party played a key role in this reorganization of higher education, and first party secretaries at all levels were given direct supervision of education.[64]

Factory life, too, continued to feel the effects of the Cultural Revolution, with some factories experiencing frequent disruptions that had their origins in the factionalism of 1966-68. Throughout the period attempts were made to reduce differences between the highest paid and lowest paid (usually apprentices). Bonuses, wage increases, and other individual material incentives were discouraged. Researchers report that the work force, particularly younger workers, lacked discipline or commitment to their jobs.[65] Promotions were made solely on the basis of seniority, and management could not fire unproductive or undisciplined workers. These inflexibilities were largely a product of the Cultural Revolution years.

The economy, recovering from the Cultural Revolution disruptions, continued to grow slowly. Increase in both industrial output and grain output had slowed down since the recovery which followed the Great Leap Forward. There were many problems: central planning had once again fallen into disarray as a result of the Cultural Revolution, and needed rejuvenation;

[62]Pepper, op. cit., p. 859.

[63]Much less emphasis has been placed on this policy since 1978, and no longer is it required that sent-down youths live permanently in the countryside.

[64]Pepper, op. cit., p. 857.

[65]William Parish, "The View from the Factory," in Ross Terrill (ed.), The China Difference (New York: Harper and Row, 1979), pp. 183-200.

without a new and massive infusion of funds, agricultural production had all but reached its limits; key industries, such as iron and steel, coal and oil, had to be modernized along with key services like transportation.[66] But part of the trouble—its root perhaps—was the unwillingness to admit the weaknesses and deal with them openly.[67] Not until the period ended in 1976 was there an admission of serious problems, such as unemployment, an admission which signified an explicit commitment to modernization.

Intense political struggle characterized 1970-76, and affected the distribution of power in provincial, district, and urban areas. The struggle quite clearly disrupted attempts to achieve integrated economic development in China. It prevented the approval of a new development plan, and only in 1976, when this struggle was resolved, could China concentrate again on a unified set of goals.

This brief outline of national-level political change in China indicates that 1970-76 was a period of intense struggle within the leadership. The issues centered around different views of economic development priorities in China, and how they should be realized. The formulation of a new Five Year Plan in 1974-75 provided a forum for this debate. On the one hand, Chiang Ch'ing, Yao Wen-yuan, Wang Hung-wen, and Chang Ch'un-chiao (later to be called the Gang of Four) demanded a continuation of Cultural Revolution policies, emphasizing self-reliance, class struggle in production and education, normative and group incentives, and increased party control, even if it meant sacrificing production and efficiency (though unwilling to admit that it did). Teng and his supporters, Li Hsien-nien and Yeh Chien-ying, saw this trend as leading to disaster and argued that only massive State intervention, reliance on intellectuals and specialists, use of individual material incentives, and more power in the hands of experts could develop China in keeping with the vision first offered by Chou En-lai in 1964, foreseeing the need for the "four modernizations" (modernization of agriculture, industry, science and technology, and the military). It is now obvious that the radicals' base of support in the country was weak. The radicals had relied chiefly on Mao's support, and with his death in September 1976 they floundered.

CONCLUSION

The story of China's development is relatively easy to review even while the reasons for particular policy decisions may be difficult to discern and an accurate assessment of policy implementation remains elusive. A fuller

---

[66] Howe, *op. cit.*, p. xxxi.

[67] *Ming Pao* (Hong Kong) reported on 14 June, 1979 that Vice-Premier Li Hsien-nien estimated that China had 20 million unemployed (in 1979).

discussion of the country's development follows in subsequent chapters, making a summary judgment on China's success in reaching its goals pointless at this stage.

The chronology of events begins with the Communists gaining control of the entire country in 1949. From that year to 1952 the CCP attempted to stabilize and gradually establish control over the economy and social institutions without, however, launching into full-scale socialism. Land reform was perhaps the most notable feature of the period, and it changed the class composition of the rural leadership in China. In urban areas the party sought to limit the independence of commercial and industrial enterprises but delayed taking direct control, thus ensuring continuity in production and distribution.

The following years, 1953-57, saw the reorganization and rapid expansion of the economy. The sector which received greatest emphasis was industry rather than agriculture, and here Soviet models of development were favored. In the countryside the formation of lower-stage and later higher-stage agricultural producers' co-operatives was intended to promote collectivization, but there was less consensus, especially among intellectuals, on the desirability of speed in that direction than Mao would have wished. An effort to win over rather than unmask the intellectuals seems to have been the motivation behind the Hundred Flowers campaign but the intellectuals were unmasked anyway when they took the slogan at its face value. Mao's move in 1957 to silence criticism by branding his opponents "rightists" ended vocal opposition for the time being, though it did not remove the cause of the dispute which stemmed from contending views on economic and social policy.

The Great Leap Forward, directed by Mao, aimed at moving China away from Soviet development strategies to an indigenous model emphasizing agriculture and small-scale industrial production, and was summarized in the policy of "walking on two legs." Mao called for the establishment of people's communes to integrate the functions of government, industry, commerce and social welfare. The commune policy had vast consequences for the rural population but had a less obvious impact in the cities. The overall effect of the 1958-59 Great Leap Forward with its decentralization of authority was immense and in many respects disastrous. China experienced a serious depression both in agriculture and industry from which it took some years to recover. A breakdown in the national economic planning system was apparent. Mao resigned as Head of State and backed away from a number of the policies he had advocated, but behind the political peace there was already evidence of a split in the leadership.

The years following the Leap were characterized by more moderate policies and systematic efforts to foster economic advancement and social progress. The incentive system was overhauled, private plots were restored, education was popularized, family planning was promoted, and so on. Some of the steps taken to solve the nation's problems were nonetheless radical, including the program to send down young people to the countryside, and the effects were far-reaching. It was the tough measures adopted to root out corruption which angered Mao, thus scratching away the veneer of peace which marked the years 1960-65. Mao attacked the office holders within the party whom he held responsible for the harsh treatment of errant cadres, accusing them of taking a capitalist road. Breaking away, he sought a power base outside the party.

The Cultural Revolution, 1966-69, was a drive for consensus and a confrontation at one and the same time. Mao's invitation to the masses to remake the country anew called for unity of purpose but his chosen instrument, the Red Guard, was meant to challenge the party establishment. The result was chaos: schools and factories closed or limped along at half strength, the economy was threatened, the nation was divided. The main violence was concentrated in the cities but suburban areas and the countryside were also affected one way or another. Some of the reforms in health, housing and education, introduced during this period, outlived the turmoil but so did much of the damage. When the army eventually restored order, power for the most part reverted in the rural areas to those who held it before the Cultural Revolution. But the radicals hung onto numerous leadership positions in the cities and within the higher levels of the party.

The years 1970-76 saw a continuation of the dispute within the leadership over development priorities and how these should be promoted. The political instability (less apparent than during the Cultural Revolution but present nonetheless) had relatively little impact on rural development. Urban areas, on the other hand, continued with radical experiments in education, commerce and industry until 1976. After the Cultural Revolution, however, institutions were restored which facilitated the reintegration of central planning. Key decisions were again being taken in Peking and, after a brief debate, economic modernization and industrial growth were singled out as the chief priority. Especially after 1976, the leadership appeared to be united around these goals, a fact which has helped the process of reintegration.

CHAPTER TWO

Factors Accounting for China's Early Success in Industrialization, 1949-76*

Tien-tung Hsueh and Pak-wai Liu

INTRODUCTION

Prior to 1949, China had long been an agrarian society with a stagnant economy in which the industrial sector played only a minor role.[1] It was not until the establishment of the People's Republic of China (PRC) that the structure of China's economy was drastically and substantially changed. Among the sectoral contributions to gross domestic product during the period under consideration (1949-76), the industrial sector ranks as the topmost one. It transformed the Chinese economy from an agriculture-dominated structure from 1965 onward.[2] The growth rate of the industrial output has been one of the highest in the world during the past two decades.

Table 1 shows the growth trend of eight selected industrial goods as far back as 1920. By and large, with the exception of crude steel and oil which grew at a fast rate in the pre-1949 period because of the low base value and the needs during war time, most of the rest of the items grew at a snail's pace with an average annual rate of about 6 per cent. The only item listed for light

---

*This chapter is part of a research project entitled, "China's Model of Development: A Sectoral Linkage Analysis" sponsored by a grant from The Chinese University of Hong Kong. Special thanks go to the Harvard-Yenching Institute, Harvard University, where T. T. Hsueh was a research fellow in 1977-78 when this chapter was in an early stage of preparation.

[1] For a discussion of the overall economic and industrial development in pre-1949 China, see P. S. Ou, "National Income of China, 1933, 1936 and 1946," *Quarterly Review of Social Sciences*, Institute of Social Sciences, Academia Sinica, Vol. 9, No. 2 (December 1947), pp. 12-30; P. S. Ou, "Revision of National Income of China, 1933," *loc. cit.*, pp. 92-153; Franklin L. Ho, "The Anatomy and Diagnosis of the Symptoms of the Chinese Economy," *Journal of Political Economy*, Nankai Institute of Economics, Vol. 4, No. 2 (January 1936), pp. 80-127; H. D. Fong, "China's Industrialization, A Statistical Survey," *Quarterly Journal of Economics and Statistics*, Nankai Institute of Economics, Vol. 1, No. 1 (March 1932), pp. 80-127 (all in Chinese).

[2] See Table A-1.

industry, cotton cloth, grew at a negative rate. In contrast, the production of industrial products in the post-1949 period, particularly crude oil and all industrial materials listed, speeded up in an astounding way. Even the production of cotton cloth has shown an impressive growth since 1949.

Right after the establishment of the People's Republic of China, the country was willing to pay almost any price to build up heavy industries during the first period of development.[3] This was perhaps the only possible quick way to establish the national capability for the production of machine tools and to strengthen the basic economic structure for reproduction. Such a strategy gave the economy a strong impetus, pushing it away from the growth trap and enabling it to take off. The turning point was the successful completion of the First Five-Year Plan when China's economy broke away from a circular-flow which characterized the pattern of growth in pre-1949 China. The initial stage of development, 1949-57, was followed immediately by the "walking on two legs" policy, which essentially extended the role taken by the central government in the course of industrialization down to the economic units at the local level. The coverage of this policy can be schematized in the following form:

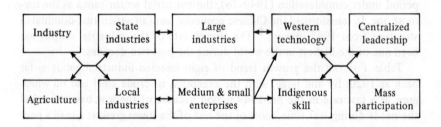

This strategy was mainly aimed at tapping the potential manpower and material resources at the local level so as to employ them to the full. In an effort to accelerate industrialization and growth, the Great Leap Forward (1958-61) was implemented. The economy was pushed beyond its limits. The result was imbalance and contraction of output. Readjustment of the economy was made in 1962-66. China continued to reshuffle her development strategy from 1967 to 1976, aiming at a balanced growth pattern. Agriculture was given more attention. However, state investment in heavy industry still took up about 50 per cent of the government budget while light industry played

[3]The classification of the three stages of China's industrial development has been elaborated in T. T. Hsueh and P. W. Liu, "Three Stages of Industrial Development in China," in *China Towards Modernization: Collected Essays for the 5th China Week* (Hong Kong: Hong Kong Federation of Students, October 1977), pp. 15-51 (in Chinese).

only a minor role.[4]

Any impression that China's industrialization has been uneventful and uniformly successful, however, should be corrected. It must be pointed out that the study of the causes for the success of China's industrialization in this chapter is mainly a long-trend analysis. If we scrutinize the time process of industrialization during the period under review, it appears that the development of China proceeded in a wave-like pattern. There were at least two retardations during the period. One occurred in some industries in 1961, as a result of mis-allocation of some resources during the Great Leap Forward, the spread of the communist wind at the expense of economic efficiency particularly in the initial period of the people's communes, the sudden withdrawal of technicians and breaking of contracts by the Russians in 1960, and the natural calamities in 1959-61. Another retardation occurred in 1967 when production and transportation were seriously disrupted during the Cultural Revolution.

But, by and large, China's industrialization between 1949 and 1976 should be considered a success, despite setbacks and reverses. Industrial growth in China was much faster than in other developing countries and faster, indeed, than in advanced industrial countries during the same period.[5] The following is a discussion of the major factors accounting for the early success of China with industrialization.

CAUSES FOR THE SUCCESS OF INDUSTRIALIZATION

1. Autonomy regarding imported materials

China commenced its industrialization at the turn of the nineteenth century. Right from the beginning her industries were dominated by external forces. For instance, foreign interests dominated ferrous metallurgy industries to the extent that they tightly controlled both production and consumption markets. During World War I foreigners disappeared temporarily from China's market. This stimulated a rapid growth in indigenous industries.[6] However, following the wind-up of the war, the market again fell under foreign domination. It was not until 1931 that tariff autonomy in China was put into effect.

---

[4] The percentage shares of the state investment in heavy and light industries were 14:1 in the third five-year plan (1966-70) and 10.2:1 in the fourth five-year plan (1971-75) in contrast to 8:1 in the first five-year plan. See special commentator "We Should Really Clarify the Objectives of Socialist Production," *Jen-min jih-pao*, Oct. 20, 1979.

[5] See Table A-2.

[6] See also H. D. Fong, *Industrial Organization in China*, Industrial Series Bulletin, No. 10, Nankai Institute of Economics, Nankai University, Tienstin, China, 1937, p. 28.

But, under an open door policy without appropriate protection measures, the development of indigenous infant industries was stifled.[7] Foreign investment distorted the domestic economy to such an extent that China could only export industrial raw materials and agricultural staples in exchange for the import of consumption and production goods. This introduced into the Chinese economy an export bias on the one hand, and import swelling and import dependence on the other. The foreign powers were driven out with the establishment of the PRC. In China's production structure, imports no longer played the role of an exogenous factor. They became a controllable variable. The government had full tariff autonomy and used it to help establish infant industries for both import and export substitution. Balance of trade could be suitably maintained and consequently indigenous industries were developed by internal initiatives and forces, in accordance with national planning.[8]

2. Rationalization of economic behavior by the collective forces[9]

The leaders of the PRC quickly launched a campaign aimed at the abolition of traditionalism and the establishment of new social institutions. The most significant change was the removal of the landlord-gentry from the upper class of society and placing the general workers in key positions for national economic reconstruction. In addition, educated youths were assigned by the authorities to work in relatively underdeveloped regions so as to make expansive development possible. Secondly, the break with feudalism, fatalism,

[7] See also Franklin L. Ho (1936), op. cit., pp. 243-248; H. D. Fong (1932), op. cit., pp. 82-85; Shih Feng-tao, "The Prospect of China's Acid and Alkali Industry," in Institute of Chinese Economic Information (ed.), Collected Essays on China's Economy, Vol. 1 (Shanghai: Life Bookstore, March 1935), pp. 65-66 (in Chinese); Shih Feng-tao, "The Crisis of China's Cotton and Linen Industry," in Collected Essays, Vol. 1, p. 89 (in Chinese); Fen Chih, "China's Match Industry," in Collected Essays, Vol. 1, pp. 67-68 (in Chinese); Hsi Chao, "The Erosion of China's National Economy by British and American Tobacco Companies," in Collected Essays, Vol. 1, pp. 97-99 (in Chinese); Ku Pao-chang, "Chemical Industry in Ten Years," in Tan Hsi-hung (ed.), Chinese Economy in Ten Years, Vol. 1 (Shanghai: Chung-hua Book Co., 1948), pp. D19, D21, D47, D51, D63 (in Chinese).

[8] For a detailed elaboration on the pattern and policy of China's foreign trade in the pre- and post-1949, see T. T. Hsueh and K. L. Shea, "China's Foreign Trade in Historical Perspective" to be published in China: Modernization and Diplomacy by the Public Affairs Research Centre in cooperation with the International Asian Studies Programme, The Chinese University of Hong Kong, 1980.

[9] See B. F. Hoselitz, "Noneconomic Factors in Economic Development," American Economic Review, Vol. 47 (May 1957), pp. 28-41; Hoselitz, "Social Implications of Economic Growth," in W. L. Johnson and D. R. Kamerschen (eds.), Readings in Economic Development (Cincinnati, Ohio: Southwestern Publishing Co., 1972), pp. 53-85.

particularism, and superstition in connection with idol worshipping so prevalent in the countryside injected a new stream of labor force into production activities on the one hand, and smashed the custom of irrational over-consumption relating to the worship of idols on the other. All these were conducive to intensive development. Some of these old social institutions which existed in pre-1949 China are shown in Table 2. Thirdly, in the First Five Year Plan period, collective organization and a spirit of daring and risk-taking were molded into the new social institutions. The extermination of the landlord-gentry class as an economic force was followed by the transformation of private land and commercial capital into national industrial capital. Collective enterprises furnished equipment and facilities for workers to play their role with the full support of the state. Thus innovation came from below, not

**Table 2.   Some Institutional Indicators in Chinese Agrarian Society
1922-25 & 1929-33**

(A)   Percentage of farmers obtaining credit (1929-33): 39%
        of which 24% for productive purposes,
                  76% for non-productive purposes

(B)   Percentage of farmers reporting conditions which affect agriculture (1929-33):
        Bad sanitation: 14%
        Superstitution: 8%
        Trouble with bandits & soldiers: 43%
        Natural calamities: 39%

(C)   Ratio of the special expenditures to net income of farmers* (1929-33):
        Weddings: 32%
        Dowries: 24%
        Birthdays: 16%
        Birth of sons: 8%
        Funerals: 26%

(D)   Percentage of families with the specified expenditure (1922-25):
        New Year holidays: 98%
        Social obligations: 74%
        Buddhism: 66%
        Local cult practices: 61%
        Education: 32%

Sources: (A) and (B): compiled from J. L. Buck, *Land Utilization in China* (New York: Council on Economic and Cultural Affairs Inc., 1956), p. 471; (C): *Ibid*, pp. 468-469; (D): Adapted from J. L. Buck, *Chinese Farm Economy* (The University of Nanking and the China Council of the Institute of Pacific Relations, 1930), p. 403.

Notes: *Net income of the farm family was estimated to be 400 Chinese ¥.

from above, and was outwardly diffused. Surveys conducted in Shanghai, Taiyuan, and Tientsin showed that, of the inventions and innovations in the first half year of 1958, the average worker contributed a share of 60 to 75 per cent.[10] The bold, pragmatic enterprise management that permeated the economic units at the lower level epitomised the spirit of China's industrialization. Moreover, it is reasonable to believe that under a collective system, the risk relating to indivisibilities and lumpiness of social overhead capital, complementarity of demand, and an uncertain supply of savings tends to be reduced to a minimum.[11] In addition, the advantage gained from external economies of high-powered linkage industries can be exploited to a greater extent, compared to the capitalistic system with its imperfectly competitive market. Table 3 provides some statistics concerning the technological progress in the industrial sector.

However, it is a pity that such a rationalization of economic behaviour fostered in the 1950s was, to a certain extent, distorted and disrupted by the ultra-leftists during the Cultural Revolution. These disruptions were caused by many factors including the magnifying of class struggle and substituting verbal criticism with violence, the inhibition of incentives by adopting a fixed wage system with little bonuses, and the practice of discretionary and sometime arbitrary actions with little regard to objective economic laws.[12]

3. Mass mobilization and better utilization of the labor force

Mass mobilization campaigns provided not only an atmosphere but, more importantly, an environment for workers to develop their potential. China has been endowed with an almost unlimited supply of labor. In an agrarian society in which the goal of people was to become government officials, land-lords or gentry, it is inevitable that, quite apart from unemployment, most of the labor force would be underutilized (see Table 4) and that working conditions would be rather poor.[13] The PRC made every attempt to enable the

[10] Yau I-hsin, "A Year of Great Achievement in Technological Revolution of the Motherland," China News, Press release, December 9, 1958, p. 16 (in Chinese).

[11] See P. N. Rosenstein-Rodan, "Notes on the Theory of the 'Big Push'" in H. S. Ellis (ed.), *Economic Development for Latin America*, International Economic Association Proceedings (London: Macmillan, 1951), pp. 57-66.

[12] See Yeh Chien-ying, "A Speech in a Ceremony Celebrating the 30th Anniversary of the Founding of the People's Republic of China," *Jen-min jih-pao*, Sept. 30, 1979; Yu Chiu-li, "The Entire Party and the Working Class of the Entire Country Mobilize and Struggle for the Dissemination of Taching-style Enterprises," *Jen-min jih-pao*, May 8, 1977.

[13] See H. D. Fong (1937) *op. cit.*, pp. 36-66; Carl Riskin, "Surplus and Stagnation in Modern China" in D. H. Perkins (ed.), *China's Modern Economy in Historical Perspective* (Stanford: Stanford University Press, 1975), pp. 69, 73-74.

Table 3.   Some Statistics on the Technical Progress
of the Industrial Sector

	1953	1957	1958-62	1963	1965	1966	1967	1976
1. Steel (varieties)	182[a]	370[a]	2,600[c]	–	–	–	–	–
2. Machine tool (varieties)	42[a]	170[a]	1,800[c]	–	–	–	–	–
3. Self-sufficient rate of steel	–	75[b]–86[k]	90[b]	–	>95[g]	–	–	–
4. Self-sufficient rate of machinery equipment	–	75[b]–60[a]	85[b]	–	–	90[h]	–	–
5. Self-sufficient rate in quantity and variety of petroleum	–	–	–	–	–	100[i]	–	–
6. Engineering technician ('000)	178[a]	802[a]	–	–	–	–	–	–
7. Qualified rate of pig iron	–	–	98[c]	99[e]	–	–	–	–
8. Qualified rate of cement	–	–	100[c]	–	–	–	–	–
9. Qualified rate of petroleum product	–	–	99[d]	99.98[f]	–	–	–	–
10. Rate of first-class quality of cotton yarn & cloth	–	–	95[c]	97[e]	–	–	–	–
11. Rate of first-class quality of steel	–	–	–	93.45[f]	–	–	–	–
12. Petroleum product of Taching oilfield (varieties)	–	–	–	–	–	–	18[j]	>40[j]

Sources: a. Chang Hsing-fu, "The Road and Method of Industrialization of Our Country," *Kung-jen jih-pao* [Worker's Daily], May 23, 1957 (in Chinese).

b. Po I-po, "Socialist Industrialization of China," *Hung-chi* [Red Flag], Vol. 20, October 22, 1963, p. 35 (in Chinese).

c. "Resolutely Perfect the Conversion of Industry onto the Track of Taking Agriculture as the Foundation," *Jen-min jih-pao*, January 3, 1963 (in Chinese).

d. "Gradually Convert Industrial Work onto the Track of Taking Agriculture as the Foundation," *Kuang-ming jih-pao*, Peking, January 21, 1963 (in Chinese).

e. Fang Chung, "The Situation of Our Country's National Economy Has Begun to Ameliorate Nationally," *Wen-hui pao*, Shanghai, September 20, 1963 (in Chinese).

f. China News (Canton), "The Chinese People Overcame Serious Natural Calamities and Economic Difficulties," Press release, August 14, 1964 (in Chinese).

g. "Eve of the Plan" from Teh Koo, Peking, *Far Eastern Economic Review*, December 23, 1965, p. 542.

h. L. K. Yung, "Self-Reliance Has Proved Itself," *China Constructions*, Vol. XV, No. 4 (April 1966), p. 8.

i. "The Great Proletarian Cultural Revolution Led Our Country's National Economy into a National New Leap Forward," *Jen-min jih-pao*, December 31, 1966 (in Chinese).
j. "In Seventeen Years Taching Oilfield Made Ten Great Contributions," *Jen-min jih-pao*, March 14, 1977 (in Chinese).
k. Kuo-chia tung-chi chu (State Statistical Bureau), "A Report on the Results of the Execution of the First Five-Year Plan (1953-1957) in Developing the National Economy," *Hsin hua pan yueh kan*, Vol. 8, p. 50 (in Chinese).

Table 4.   Non-Agricultural Labor Force in 1933* and Possible Transference after 1949

	% share of total non-agricultural labor force	Compared with the labor productivity of factory manufacture (100%)	Possible transference after 1949
1. Mining	2.24%	0.48	
2. Factory manufactures	2.41%	1.00	
3. Handicrafts	30.37%	0.20	(A)
4. Construction	3.70%	0.27	
5. Traditional transportation	9.40%	0.24	(A)
6. Modern transportation and communications	1.13%	1.73	
7. Trade	19.60%	0.47	
8. Peddlers	7.41%	0.33	(A)
9. Finance, banking and insurance	0.47%	1.94	
10. Monk, lama, priest and other liberal profession	3.87%	0.20	(B)
11. Servants	7.65%	0.08	(B)
12. Public administration	11.75%	0.25	

Source: Gee-hung Diang, "An Estimate of the Working Population of China," *Quarterly Review of Social Science*, Vol. 9, No. 2, Dec. 1947, p. 89 (in Chinese).

Notes: (A) reorganized into the collective form with more equipment and facilities. Some of handicrafts were transfered to factory manufactures.
   (B) exterminated; most of them were transfered to other occupations.
   *   Non-agricultural labor force was estimated at 45,914,000 persons.

labor force to work in a fuller capacity, and to release the female labor force from the bondage of feudal society. As a result, the labor force constituted an abundant input in the production function and became a substitute for relatively scarce capital goods. Towards the end of 1954, the government was able to absorb and to reallocate some 2.4 million unemployed people,[14] and the unemployment problem was basically solved by the end of 1957.[15] It has been estimated that as many as 90 million people joined the front in the production of steel and iron in the Great Leap Forward years. Nearly all people in every district and commune actively took part in industrial reconstruction. (See, for example, Tables A-3 and A-4 in Appendix.) As a result, local production units initiated small factories producing chemicals, insecticides, and chemical fertilizers; they established small machine factories repairing agricultural tools and manufacturing simple machinery and ball bearings; and they started small coal mines and electric stations. The prominent role played by medium and small industries in China's industrialization is partly shown in Table 5. The better absorption and utilization of the abundant labor force thus played an important part in the acceleration of industrialization.[16]

However, as a consequence of the stability of the economy and the promotion of public health facilities, the growth rate of population was about 2 per cent or more in the period under consideration. This swelled the labor force tremendously. The employment problem was aggravated by the fact that the state budget invested too much in heavy industry[17] which absorbed relatively less labor. The burden of labor absorption then rested on the development of the communes and the street industries. In fact, with the masses of youth waiting for jobs, one way to solve the employment problem was to dispatch the reserve army to the countryside. Towards the late 1970s, the problem

[14] See "Gradually Eliminate the Unemployment Phenomenon," *Ta-kung pao* (Tienstin), October 4, 1955.

[15] See State Statistical Bureau, *Ten Great Years* (Peking: Foreign Languages Press, 1960), p. 177; and also L. G. Reynolds, *et al., Observations on the Chinese Economy*, New Haven, December 1, 1973.

[16] See also John C. H. Fei and G. Ranis, *Development of the Labor Surplus Economy: Theory and Policy* (Homewood, Ill.: Richard D. Irwin, 1964), pp. 111-150.

[17] Some data of the state investment on the various sectors as a fraction of the government budget are shown as follows:

Investment on	First Five-Year Period	1978	1979
Agriculture	7.8%	10.7%	14%
Light industry	5.9%	5.4%	5.8%
Heavy Industry	46.5%	54.7%	46.8%

Sources: Liu Sui-nien and Chou Yung, "To Deal Correctly with the Ratio between Accumulation and Consumption," *Jen-min jih-pao*, May 1, 1979; Yu Chiu-li, "A Report on the Draft National Economic Plan, 1979," *Jen-min jih-pao*, June 29, 1979.

Table 5. Some Statistics on the Distribution of Large, Medium and Small Industries

	1959	1965	1966	1972	1973	1975
Distribution of the enterprises:						
Large enterprise	–	20%[b]	–	–	–	–
Medium and small enterprises	–	80%[b]	–	–	–	–
Share of medium & small enterprises:						
Cement	–	20%[b]	–	48%[d]	50%[e]	57%[g]
Coal	40%[a]	30%[b]	–	>30%[f]	–	–
Chemical fertilizer	–	40%[b]	–	–	–	69%[f]
Resultant ammonia	–	–	–	–	50%[e]	–
Pig iron	>50%[a]	–	–	–	–	–
Steel	>1/3[a]	–	–	–	–	–
Gross product of agricultural machinery	–	–	2/3[c]	–	–	–
Hydroelectric power	–	–	–	16%[d]	–	–

Sources: a. Wu Chun-yang, "The Great Meaning of Completing the Second Five-Year Plan Three Years Ahead of Schedule," *Jen-min jih-pao*, February 10, 1960 (in Chinese).

b. China News (Canton), "The Policy of Self-Reliance Brought Great and Deep Changes to Industrial Production and Construction in China," Press release, Vol. 3963, February 2, 1965 (in Chinese).

c. R. Kojima, "Self-sustained National Economy in Mainland China," *Developing Economy*, March 1967, p. 64.

d. N. R. Chen, "Industrial Development in Mainland China," *Asian Affairs*, May–June 1975, p. 291.

e. China News (Canton), "Our Country's Achievement in Developing Socialist Industries in a Self-Reliant Way," Press release, Vol. 6905, 1973 (in Chinese).

f. "Our Country's Economy Develops at a High Speed. Grain Output Reaches Target One Year Ahead of Schedule," *Ta-kung pao*, Hong Kong, June 13, 1976 (in Chinese).

g. CIA, USA (1976), *op. cit.*, p. 24.

became more serious because some disguised unemployed moved back to the cities from the countryside.[18] The authorities were fully aware of the seriousness of this. The expansion and creation of the service sector, the promotion of light industries and the transfer of the labor force back again to the countryside were measures taken by the government to solve the employment problem.

4. Control of consumption and effective channelling of savings into investment

The level of consumption was effectively controlled by the authorities in at least three ways:[19] (1) Rationing and price discrimination policies were adopted for certain commodities based on the situation of their supply; (2) Social welfare schemes were provided for workers through which some savings were collected; (3) A relatively slow increase in the wage bill which fell behind the increase in labor productivity enabled the accumulation of retained earnings in communes and state enterprises.[20] As a result, the non-essential personal consumption of the high income class in pre-1949 China was reduced to a minimum. One estimate shows that the ratio of potential economic surplus above mass consumption to net domestic product in 1933 was as high as 36.8 per cent.[21] Moreover, because of the numerous investment programs carried out by the PRC, it was possible to channel all the surpluses into capital construction activities through an effective banking and financial system.

Under the circumstances of little foreign aid and loans and no foreign investment in this period, the high rate of investment in the post-1949 period was almost all due to the rapid growth of domestic savings and their effective

[18]To the best of our knowledge, there are few unemployment data officially published by the PRC. *Jen-min jih-pao* of July 20, 1979 reported a figure of 7 million job-waiting workers, quoting from a talk given by Hsueh Mu-chiao. Some sinologists have surmised that the unemployment figure was as high as 20 million (see *Sing-tao jih-pao*, Hong Kong, July 30, 1979). Interviews with those who left the PRC suggest that the unemployment may be voluntary, or due to desertion from the countryside to the city, or the refusal of jobs assigned by the government.

[19]See also T. J. Hughes and D.E.T. Luard, *The Economic Development of Communist China* (London: Oxford University Press, 1962), pp. 186-197; D. H. Perkins, *Market Control and Planning in Communist China* (Cambridge, Massachusets: Harvard University Press, 1966), pp. 99-116.

[20]The average growth rate of wages during 1952-56 was 33.5 per cent. However, that of labor productivity of the state industrial sector reached 70.4 per cent. See Chou En-lai, *A Report on the Proposal of the Second Five-Year Plan in Developing the National Economy* (Peking: Jen-min chu-pan she, 1956), p. 32 (in Chinese); see also C. Howe, *Wage Patterns and Wage Policy in Modern China, 1919-1972* (London: Cambridge University Press, 1973), pp. 28-54.

[21]See Carl Riskin (1975), *op. cit.*, pp. 72-77.

transformation into capital formation.[22] Some of the information is given in Table 6 (see also Table A-5 in Appendix). Since 1968, all domestic government bonds and interest were paid back. The public sector operated steadily without foreign and domestic debts.

As shown in Table 6, the rate of capital formation experienced a rapid jump from 7.5 per cent in pre-1949 to 20 per cent or more in post-1949. The percentage went higher still in more recent years. One can see that an enormous portion of the investment was allocated to the industrial sector. It increased from 45.5 per cent in 1952 to 62.1 per cent in 1957, and there was no sign of decline during the 1960s and the 1970s.

In order to make China a truly independent country both politically and economically, the PRC devoted much of its effort to the increase of reproduction capacity. As shown in Table 7, the share of producer goods in total industrial output rose from 33.9 per cent in 1949-51 to 58.1 per cent in 1973-75. Throughout the whole period, the output of producer goods grew as much as three times faster than that of consumer goods.

As a consequence of over expansion of investment in producer goods, a structural imbalance emerged in the economy particularly in the latter half of the 1970s. Even though the investment was heavily biased in favour of basic construction in heavy industry, the economy was confronted with a severe shortage in some important complementary inputs such as fuel, electricity, finished steel, building materials and transportation services. The result was a serious problem in disproportion in factor allocation. Moreover, the tremendous increase in producer goods was at the expense of consumer goods which declined in share. The welfare and the work incentive of the workers were negatively affected to a great extent.[23]

5. Moral incentives and X-efficiency

Last but not least, the workers' enthusiasm for the many patriotic campaigns during national reconstruction should be noted. For more than a century China was invaded and disgraced by foreign military and economic powers. The workers, and particularly the cadres, have a deep sense of responsibility

[22] For pre-1949, see H. D. Fong, *Industrial Capital in China*, Industrial Series Bulletin, No. 9, Nankai Institute of Economics, Nankai University, Tientsin, China, April 1936; in particular, pp. 39-41, 65-68.

[23] See Yu Chiu-li, "The Development Situation of Our National Economy," *Jen-min jih-pao*, Oct. 25, 1977; Li Cheng-jui and Chang Cho-yuan, "Growing Truly at High Speed Requires Growing by Proportion," *Jen-min jih-pao*, March 16, 1979; Yao Ping, "If Adjustment Is Well Done, Development Will Be Rapid," *Jen-min jih-pao*, April 17, 1979; and special commentator, *Jen-min jih-pao*, Oct. 20, 1979.

Table 6.   Some Statistics on Investment and Savings

(A) INVESTMENT:

    (i) Gross domestic capital formation/Gross domestic product (%):

        1933: 7.3   1952: 19.5   1954: 24.4   1956: 26.8   1960s: about 20
        1931-36: 7.5 1953: 23.8   1955: 24.5   1957: 23.5   1970s: 27.9-28.6

    (ii) Share of fixed investment in industry (%)*:

        1952: 45.5   1954: 57.8   1956: 56.1
        1953: 54.1   1955: 56.2   1957: 62.1

(B) SAVINGS:

	1951-52	1953-57	1965-71	1970-71	1976-77
(i) National private savings (%):†	58.4[a]	@28.2[a]	–	–	–
(ii) Saving deposits (%):†					
National total	–	–	–	14.0[c]	–
Urban	57.3[b]	@26.8[b]	–	14.0[c]	10.5[d]
Rural	–	–	@11.2[c]	–	19.2[d]
Collective	–	–	@13.1[c]	–	–
Individual	–	–	@ 4.7[c]	–	–

    (iii) Fixed savings/Total deposits (%)[e]: 1952: 46.6   1957: 70.3   1963: 82.5

Sources: (A) Of the investment data, that in the 60s is from D. Davis, "Interview with Han Suyin," *Far Eastern Economic Review*, Nov. 24, 1966, p. 430, and those in the 70s are from D. H. Perkins (ed.), *China's Modern Economy in Historical Perspective*, p. 165 in 1957 constant prices; the rest are from K. C. Yeh, "Capital Formation," chapter 8 in A. Eckstein, W. Galenson, and T. C. Liu (eds.), *Economic Trends in Communist China* (Chicago: Aldine Publishing Co., 1968), p. 511 in 1952 constant prices for (A)(i) and p. 541 in current prices for (A)(ii).

        (B) Savings: a. *Ta-kung pao* (Peking), March 19, 1958.
                b. State Statistical Bureau, *Ten Great Years*, p. 219.
                c. Leo Goodstadt, "The Hunt for Affluence," *Far Eastern Economic Review*, May 13, 1972, p. 42.
                d. *Jen-min jih-pao*, Jan. 9, 1978.
                e. Kao Yu, "On People's Savings under Socialist System," *Ching-chi tao-pao*, June 15, 1964, p. 42.

Note: *Denominator covers fixed investment in agriculture, industry, transportation, trade, and finance.
       †Annual growth rate.

Table 7.   Structure and Growth of Producer and Consumer Goods

| | Growth Trend | | % Share | |
	Producer goods	Consumer goods	Producer goods	Consumer goods
1949-51	100.0	100.0	33.9	66.1
1952-54	233.8	192.0	38.4	61.6
1956-57	384.6	245.5	44.5	55.5
1958-60	918.7	323.2	59.5	40.7
1961-63	627.7	242.9	57.0	43.0
1964-66	987.7	467.9	51.9	48.1
1967-69	1,113.8	575.0	49.8	50.2
1970-72	1,860.0	749.1	56.0	44.0
1973-75	2,540.0	936.6	58.1	41.9

Sources: a. CIA, USA (1976), op. cit., p. 17.
            b. State Statistical Bureau, Ten Great Years, p. 87.

Notes: These are compiled from the indices of industrial production in source (a) by
            plugging in the actual figures of producer and consumer goods in 1957 provided
            by source (b).

and devotion to their country. The ship *Yau-Tsin* constructed within only 58
working days in 1958 is one of many achievement of the workers, where the
incentive was largely patriotism.[24] The motivation, which can be categorized
as X-efficiency, may be in some cases far more important than allocative
efficiency.[25]

During the 1950s there were many campaigns. There was the "Three
Oppositions Campaign" which was directed against corruption, extravagance
and bureaucratization. The "Five Oppositions Campaign" was against bribery,
smuggling and tax evasion, theft of national wealth, scamping work and
lessening the quantity of materials, and theft of national intelligence information.[26] In the 1960s, the "Agriculture Learn from Tachai" and the "Industry
Learn from Taching" campaigns established prototypes for other economic

[24] See Yao I-hsin (1958), op. cit., p. 15.

[25] See H. Leibenstein, "Allocative Efficiency vs. X-Efficiency," American Economic
Review, Vol. 56 (June 1966), pp. 392-415.

[26] See also Hsueh Mu-chiao, Su Hsing, and Lin Tzu-li, Socialist Transformation of the
Chinese National Economy (Peking: Jen-min chu-pan-she, 1978), pp. 33-34 (in Chinese);
Institute of Economic Research, Social Science Council of China, Socialist Transformation of the Chinese Capitalistic Industry and Commerce (Peking: Jen-min chu-pan-she,
1978), pp. 124-142.

units to emulate. The "Ten-Nays" were proclaimed as the "Taching Spirit."[27]

The campaigns were designed to heighten the morale of the general workers, to establish a venturesome spirit in the rank and file, and to eradicate corruption among officials. In general, a more favorable social environment for innovation and economic development was fostered in the early period. However, it was inevitable that in some cases where the campaign got away from the original objectives, it had a demoralizing effect on the bureaucracy and the intellectuals. They were less likely to take initiative for fear of criticisms and political consequences. Also, since the Cultural Revolution, bureaucratic management, extreme egalitarianism, and the slow rise in the living standard had some demoralizing effects on the workers and the peasants. This has to be overcome if China wants to push forward her industrialization program.

As a summary of the key factors mentioned above, it might be helpful to present, by means of a diagram, the factors contributing toward the acceleration of industrialization after 1949.

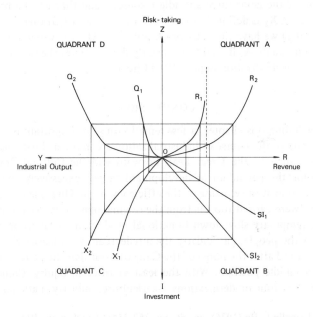

Figure 1.   Comparison of pre- and post-1949 industrialization

[27] The "Ten-Nays" are as follows: not afraid of misery, not afraid of death, not for fame, not for selfish interests, no dispute on working conditions, no dispute on work time, no dispute on work rewards, no discrimination between positions, no dispute on work loads, no distinction between the front line and the rear.

Let us start off with quadrant A. R designates the risk-revenue curve in which the extent of risk implies also the frontier of investment and the dimensions of production activity. Subscript 1 stands for pre-1949, and subscript 2 for post-1949. In the pre-1949 period, the rich usually converted windfall gains into gold, jewellery, and land. Therefore, quite a large portion of industrial and commercial capital eventually flowed back as land capital and idle hoarding. This makes the risk-revenue frontier rather narrow as shown in R_1. Old social institutions were replaced by new collective organizations and value systems in post-1949 China, as described earlier. R_2, therefore, has a broader frontier than R_1. Quadrant B shows that the banking system, which channelled savings into investment, was not as sound in pre-1949 China as in post-1949 China.[28] The post-1949 revenue-investment (savings) function SI_2 is much more expansionary in terms of OR (see Table 6). In quadrant C, one can see that given an unlimited supply of labor, the only bottleneck factor is capital and X in fact implies the industrial production function. Since the PRC devoted all its effort towards economic reconstruction, through better utilization of the labor force and idle resources, and through the promotion of technology, X_2 is definitely more outward in terms of OI than X_1. Finally, in quadrant D we have the activity-output curve Q_1, Q_2 which is simply the result of quadrants A, B, and C. Q_2 clearly demonstrates the phenomenon of success in industrialization in post-1949 China.

CONCLUSION

In concluding this chapter, a few remarks on some important issues which occurred during the course of industrialization are in order. First, the massive campaigns, such as the Great Leap Forward and the Cultural Revolution, often swung the pendulum of development targets excessively towards the equity criterion at the expense of the efficiency norm. On some occasions the campaigns were carried too far from the original objectives. As a result, apart from the temporary slow-down in national production, a far from negligible portion of the people, particularly the intellectuals, were negatively affected. It was not until after the purge of the Gang of Four that the pendulum swung back to a middle position. With the least sacrifice in equity, China is now promoting her four modernizations—agriculture, industry, national defense,

[28] See Franklin L. Ho (1936), *op. cit.*, pp. 252-254; Chou Wen-pin, "The Significance of the Abnormal Development of China's Economy in the Current Stage," in Institute of Chinese Economic Information (ed.), *Collected Essays on China's Economy*, Vol. 1 (March 1935), pp. 5-7 (in Chinese); Hsu Hsueh-han, "High Interest Loan in Chinese Villages," in Institute of Chinese Economic Information (ed.), *Collected Essays on China's Economy*, Vol. 2 (December 1935), pp. 138-145 (in Chinese).

and science and technology—essentially based on the efficiency norm.

Secondly, the key policy for industrial development at present places the emphasis on intensification which involves specialization, cooperation, and coordination in and among industries in order to gain economies of scale, quality control, technological progress, and scientific management.[29] It should be noted that the present intensification policy is simply a logical consequence of the past effort at extension by scattering small and comprehensive industries down to the local level. As a matter of fact, the achievement of economic development arises from both the product of the extension and the intensification effects, neither of which should be neglected.

Lastly, there were cyclical fluctuations of industrial policy during the period under review. Emphasis was placed on a policy of moderate extension during 1949-57, and on a policy of extreme extension in 1958-61. The emphasis then changed to a policy of intensification during 1962-66. A policy of extension was again implemented in 1967-76, which was followed by a policy of intensification after 1976. The evidence shows that a policy of extension was usually accompanied by an overemphasis on politics at the expense of economic efficiency.

[29] See Hu Chiao-mu, "Operate according to Economic Laws to Accelerate the Realization of the Four Modernizations," *Jen-min jih-pao*, Oct. 6, 1978.

APPENDIX

Table A-1. Sectoral Contribution to Gross Domestic Product[1]

	1933		1936[a]	1946[a]	1952[c]	1955[c]	1957[d]	1962[d]	1965[d]	1971[d]
	Ou[a]	L-Y[b]								
Agricultural sector (%)	67.7	70.9	70.8	68.7	59.2	52.9	51.2	39.8	39.5	33.7
Industrial sector[2] (%)	12.6	12.7	12.6	7.8	21.0	27.4	28.2	39.5	39.9	45.7
Transportation, Trade and Finance (%)	19.7	16.4	16.6	23.5	19.8	19.8	20.6	20.6	20.6	20.6
Actual figures	18,604	26,460	23,507	16,722	61.13	78.80	85.85	87.03	122.15	179.00
Unit	million ¥	million ¥	million ¥	million ¥ in 1933 prices	billion ¥ in 1952 prices		billion ¥ in 1957 prices			

Sources:
a. Pao-san Ou, "National Income of China, 1933, 1936 and 1946," *Quarterly Review of Social Sciences*, Vol. 9, No. 2, Dec. 1947, p. 19.

b. T. C. Liu and K. C. Yeh, *The Economy of the Chinese Mainland: National Income and Economic Development, 1933-1959* (Princeton, New Jersey: Princeton University Press, 1965), p. 66.

c. S. Ishikawa, *National Income and Capital Formation in Mainland China* (Tokyo: Institute of Asian Economic Affair, 1965), pp. 76-77.

d. D. H. Perkins, "Growth and Changing Structure of China's Twentieth Century Economy," in D. H. Perkins (ed.), *China's Modern Economy in Historical Perspective* (Stanford, California: Stanford University Press, 1975), p. 161.

Notes: [1] Gross domestic product here simply follows the socialist definition which, with the exception of transportation, trade and finance, excludes the service sector.
[2] Industrial sector covers mining, manufacturing, and construction.

Table A-2.   Industrial Growth of Selected Large Countries

Average growth rate	China	India	USSR	USA	Japan	Brazil	Mexico	UK	France
1938-48	–	–	–	8.3	–9.1	–	–	1.0	0.2
1939-48	–	1.5	–	–	–	6.4	–	–	–
1940-50	–	–	5.7	–	–	–	–	–	–
1950-60	24.1	6.8	11.8	3.8	16.5	9.2	6.2	3.0	6.5
1962-71	14.4	5.0	8.3	4.5	12.1	–	8.5	2.9	6.0
1962-70	–	–	–	–	–	6.6	–	–	–

Sources: China, gross value of industrial output in 1957 *yuan*.

1950-57: adopted from The State Statistical Bureau (SSB) of the People's Republic of China, *Ten Great Years* (Peking: Foreign Languages Press, 1960), p. 87.

1964-66 and 1968-71: adopted frm Central Intelligence Agency (CIA) of the United States, National Foreign Assessment Center, *China: Gross Value of Industrial Output 1965-1977* (Washington, D.C., June 1978), p. 8.

1958-63 and 1967: adopted and interpolated with the industrial production index appearing the CIA (U.S.A.), *People's Republic of China: Handbook of Economic Indicators* (Washington, D.C., August 1976), p. 3.

The rest of the countries: obtained from United Nations, *The Growth of World Industry 1938-1961, National Tables* (New York, 1963); United Nations, *The Growth of World Industry*, 1972 edition, Vol. 1; *General Industrial Statistics, 1962-1971* (New York, 1974).

Table A-3.   Shenyang's Street Industry, 1975

No. of factory:	2,490
Employee:	170,000; 80% Female
Output:	10.4% of total city industrial products
Promotion:	400 were promoted to be city enterprises
Growth:	1975/1966 = 900%
Self-sufficient rate:	(1) Light industry products from 30% up to 80%
	(2) Small agricultural instruments: 100%
Products:	Machine tool, automobile parts, electric motor, transformer, T.V., electronic and medical instruments, agricultural machinery, daily articles, other metallurgical parts, construction, military and wireless etc.

Markets:	Domestic:	(1)	large enterprise
		(2)	agriculture
		(3)	light industry
	Foreign:	(1)	exports
		(2)	foreign aids

Source: Chung-wen, "The Street Industry of Shenyang," *Ta-kung pao*, Hong Kong, December 1, 1976 (in Chinese).

Table A-4.   Tsun-Hua District's Commune Industry, 1969-76

	1969	1970	1976
(1) No. of enterprise			
(a) District-governed	31		48 (Among them, 26 were scaled up)
(b) Commune-governed			299
(2) Total output	base		390%
(3) Products			
(a) District-governed			Steel & iron, plastic, paper, industrial and fine arts, bicycle parts, weld etc.
(b) Commune-governed			Steel & iron, coal, cement, chemical fertilizer, threshing machine, harvester, ball bearings, simple machine tool, cotton yarn, cotton cloth, sugar etc.
(4) No. of production teams			
(a) District			692 mainly for repair and
(b) Commune			3,384 maintenance
(5) % increase in		base	
Enterprise			130%
Employee			200%
Value of product			280%
Net revenue			400%
(6) Tractor-cultivated area/Total area			73.5%

Source: "Promulgate the Spirit of 'chung pang tzu', Let the Flowers of Taching Blossom among *Hsien* and Commune Industries," *Jen-min jih-pao*, May 16, 1977 (in Chinese).

Table A-5.   Interest Rate per Annum on Loan
in the Pre- and Post-1949 China

PRE-1949
Interest rate on loan in the rural areas

Province	Prefecture (Nos. of village)	Lowest	Ordinary	Highest
Kwangsi[a]	Tsang-wu (4)	14%	24%	32%
	I-ning (3)	44%	56%	60%
	Liu-chou (5)	36%	39%	48%
Yunnan[b]	Lu-feng (6)	25%	40%	70%
	Kai-yuan (2)	10%	35%	45%
Szechuan[c]	Pawnshops in 15 prefectures	30%	–	50%

POST-1949
Interest rate on loan from the People's Bank[d]

	1953	1955	1958	1959	1972
Industrial loans					
State and public-private joint enterprises	5.04-16.80	5.76-8.64	7.20	7.20	5.04
Private enterprises	10.8-19.8	10.8-11.88	8.64	–	–

Average growth rate of the industrial loans from the People's Bank[e]

1952-57	1957-64
@ >32%	@ 24.2%

Sources: a. Council for Rural Reconstruction, Executive Yuan, *Farm Survey in Kwangsi Province* (Shanghai: The Commercial Press, 1935), p. 243 (in Chinese).

b. ————, *Farm Survey in Yunnan Province* (Shanghai: The Commercial Press, 1935), pp. 174, 273 (in Chinese).

c. Lu Ping-teng, *Farm Economy in Szechuan* (Shanghai: The Commercial Press, 1936), p. 449 (in Chinese).

d. Interest rates in 1953-59 are from K. H. Hsiao, *Money and Monetary Policy in Communist China* (New York: Columbia University Press, 1971), p. 130; and that in 1972 is from C. Howe, *China's Economy* (London: Paul Elek Book Ltd. 1978), p. 58.

e. China News (Canton), Press release, April 18, 1965, pp. 9-10.

CHAPTER THREE

Commune Education and Rural Development in China

Pedro Pak-tao Ng

INTRODUCTION

China is predominantly a rural country with over 80 per cent of its population living and working in the countryside. Although its productivity and standard of living on the whole are still quite some distance behind the world's developed economies, China, during the last three decades or so under a Communist government, has managed to produce sufficiently for its people, to provide them adequately with health, educational, and various welfare services, and in effect to enhance the general quality of life to a degree unheard of, and indeed impossible, before 1949.

China has made considerable progress in material terms, but this is only half the story. The other half lies in the fact that the human factor has been highly important in bringing about what China has achieved in its rural development. As is well known, China's rural development since 1958 has proceeded mainly through the design of the people's commune which has effectively implemented China's collectivized mode of production. The success of the communes rests heavily on the human factor, for collectivization requires ideological commitment and mass mobilization. A country's educational system is directly involved in creating and shaping the kind of human factor considered appropriate for the country's development. In the case of China, education is regarded as a strategic instrument not only for transmitting the knowledge and skills necessary for China's development but also for cultivating the new "socialist man" who has both the culture and the socialist consciousness so vital for building China into a strong socialist country.[1] Education is therefore highly purposive and instrumental. In China, as in many developing countries,

[1] The idea that education is to create new "socialist men," which gained great prominence after the Cultural Revolution, was elaborated upon by Mao Tse-tung in one of his most important policy-making speeches, "On the Correct Handling of Contradictions among the People," first published in 1957. *The Selected Works of Mao Tse-tung* (Peking: Foreign Languages Press, 1977), Vol. 5, pp. 384-421.

education plays a very important role in social, economic, and political development. This importance is perhaps much greater in China than in other developing countries, both at the normative or ideal level and in practice. In the following pages we shall examine the role of education in China's rural development.[2] What are China's developmental tasks in building and transforming its rural, agricultural economy? How are these tasks performed by the commune system? Given these developmental tasks, what are the characteristics of China's rural education? What are the consequences of education for rural development? These are some of the questions which must be addressed.

TASKS OF RURAL DEVELOPMENT IN CHINA

The basic strategy in China's economic development since the 1960s is that "agriculture is the foundation while industry is the leading factor."[3] This is

[2] In writing this chapter, the author has drawn upon his observations during a field tirp taken in December 1976 to two rural communes in Guangdong province, namely, Huancheng Commune (population: 59,000) of Xinhui County and Dali Commune (population: 68,000) of Nanhai County. This field trip was conducted by a group of social scientists from The Chinese University of Hong Kong, as part of the research project entitled, "The Commune and Socio-economic Development in Communist China." The project is carried out under the auspices of the University's Social Research Centre with guidance from Prof. C. K. Yang of the Sociology Department of Pittsburgh University and is supported by funds from the Trustees of Lingnan University. Since 1976-77 social and political conditions in China have undergone considerable changes because of the country's current drive for modernization. Certain aspects of rural education have changed accordingly. The present official position on educational policy basically demands a closer relationship between education and economic development. The essence of this new policy is contained in Vice-Premier Deng Xiaoping's address delivered at the National Conference for Educational Work on April 22, 1978. See *Renmin Ribao* [People's Daily], "Address at the National Conference of Educational Work" (April 26, 1978). Other sources describing recent changes in Chinese education include: Suzanne Pepper, "An Interview on Changes in Chinese Education after the 'Gang of Four'," *China Quarterly*, No. 72 (December 1977), pp. 815-824; *China Reconstructs*, "What's Happening in China's Education?" (April 1978); and Pedro Pak-tao Ng, "Open-Door Education in the Chinese Communes: Rationale, Problems, and Recent Changes," forthcoming in *Modern China*.

[3] The basic idea underlying this slogan can be traced to Mao Tse-tung's essay "On the Ten Relationships," written in 1956. *Selected Works of Mao*, Vol. 5, pp. 284-307. The dual emphasis given to both agriculture and industry, treating the former as "base," began to be implemented in the 1960s as a policy readjustment, following the difficulties of the Great Leap Forward. A great deal has been written on this. See, for example, Keith Buchanan, *The Transformation of the Chinese Earth* (London: G. Bells and Sons, 1970), pp. 231-235; A. Doak Barnett, *Uncertain Passage: China's Transition to the Post-Mao Era* (Washington, D. C.: The Brookings Institution, 1974), pp. 124-127; Alexander Eckstein, *China's Economic Revolution* (Cambridge: Cambridge University Press, 1977), pp. 60-61; and Maurice Meisner, *Mao's China: A History of the People's Republic* (New York: The Free Press, 1977), pp. 274-276.

essentially in accordance with the principle of "walking on two legs" advocated ever since the Great Leap Forward. While large-scale industries are generally concentrated in the urban areas and play a major role in China's industrialization development, the livelihood of China's huge population depends heavily on raising the productivity of agriculture in China's vast countryside. To develop agriculture, however, from the impoverished and chaotic situation of three decades ago required extensive institutional transformation and in effect a reconstruction of China's rural society. Such reconstruction consists of political, social, cultural, technical, and physical changes.

Political changes.   Although land ownership and the mode of production have long been changed from a fragmentary, landlord-dominated and un-coordinated situation to a centrally coordinated but locally self-administered collectivized system, a major task of rural development is the continuing and growing institutionalization of various socialist practices to make collectivization work in the interest of the peasantry. The socialization of the rural masses for their participation in and acceptance of such basic socialist values as "self-reliance" and "serve the people" is in many ways a political socialization process.[4] The institutionalization of propaganda teams and activities and the integration of formal education with productional activities promote the process. The commune is the structural framework for implementing the social and political changes accompanying a collectivized mode of production.

Social and cultural changes.   In traditional China social relationships were typically kinship-oriented, and loyalties were also largely kinship-determined. Highly earth-bound in life style, the peasantry was traditionally conservative in outlook, slow to change its folk beliefs and technology, or to introduce innovative ways of thinking. All this is unsuitable for developing a forward-looking collective economy. Social relationships in the context of a much broader collective system, and commitment to collective needs have to be cultivated. Old values and thinking, such as those denigrating the worth of manual labor or depriving women of their rightful status in society, must be criticized and replaced by new socialist values emphasizing social equality. Thus, for example, the planned births campaign, actively carried out in both rural and urban areas since the early 1970s, is an attempt to control population growth mainly through an intensive appeal to the new values and beliefs which advocate the participation of women in the labor force. The change in values is seen as necessary to bring about a new outlook in life among the peasants. The quality of peasants in terms of skill, capacity for rational thinking, and receptivity to innovation is to be improved, partly through formal education

---

[4]For a discussion of "self-reliance," see, for example, Alexander Eckstein, *op. cit.*, pp. 284-285; and for "serve the people," see A. Doak Barnett, *op. cit.*, pp. 13-14.

and partly through the provision of various "cultural" services and activities. The intention is to provide the peasants with opportunities to use their experience and skills to help others, e.g., teaching agricultural knowledge in schools. Consequently, their life is enriched by diversifying their experiences and broadening their social and political horizons. They are systematically socialized in the collective way of life and are encouraged to have a role, however small it may be, in the operation and improvement of the production team or brigade of which they are part. Their contribution, not only as farmers doing repetitive work but also as enlightened and dedicated commune members, is seen as vital in making the whole commune system work.

Technical changes. Given China's immense population and yet relatively scarce cultivable land, there is a limit to agricultural productivity, however much the rural labor force input can be, unless agricultural technology is improved. The needed technical changes include: better utilization of land, scientific application of fertilizers, improvements in water control and management, rational approaches to planting, improved seeds, and of course mechanization. To facilitate these tasks, China thinks it important to build up various rural industries utilizing local raw materials and resources to produce machinery and other inputs for agricultural development. These industries play a significant role in bringing about the technical changes necessary for raising agricultural productivity and also, as the rural economy is diversified, for increasing employment opportunities and improving the rural population's standard of living.[5]

Physical changes. Closely related to technical changes are changes in the physical appearance of the rural areas. Thus, for instance, the lay-out of cultivated fields has to be rearranged in such a way as to facilitate more effective irrigation and maximization of planting. New cultivable land needs to be created by reclamation or removing hills and grading the surface of fields for proper irrigation and drainage. Besides, what used to be merely simple villages has to be organized in the commune system which requires the incorporation into the rural scene of a variety of amenities and facilities such as health clinics, schools, banks, shops, factories and workshops, many of which are needed to support agricultural development. Roads and pathways need to be expanded to link together the constituent parts of a commune. These are all important to provide better conditions in which agriculture may develop and on which enhancement of the quality and hence the attractiveness of rural life depends.

[5] Sartaj Aziz, *Rural Development: Learning from China* (London: Macmillan, 1978), pp. 52-53.

THE COMMUNE AS A MODEL OF DEVELOPMENT

From the above description of the tasks of rural development it can be seen that, from China's point of view, rural development requires a comprehensive approach aimed at introducing fundamental changes touching on practically all aspects of rural life. In effect, the concept of "rural" is greatly modified to mean much more than "agricultural." It is meant to incorporate many elements of industrialization and modernization so that the rural areas should no longer be, as they were in the pre-Communist days, places plagued by hardship and poverty. Instead, the intention is to change rural areas into places full of productive vigor and hence able to attain their due share of progress and prosperity.

The people's commune is China's basic and unique model of rural development.[6] There are now approximately 50,000 communes in China. The average commune today has some 14,000 people divided into 15 production brigades which are subdivided into roughly 100 production teams[7] There are variations, however. Thus, a commune in a remote mountainous region may consist of several thousand people, while communes in Guangdong province, for example, may have anywhere from 20,000 to 50,000 people.[8] The basic rationale for formation of the communes lies in the desire to organize and mobilize energies and resources on a large scale to implement the tasks of rural development.

The commune system consists of three structural levels, each with its specific purposes and functions. The lowest level, the production team, usually consists of a natural village and is the basic production and accounting unit. Income is distributed, after paying state taxes, through a workpoint system which takes into account not only individuals' but also the collectivity's work contribution. The production team also engages in certain investment activities for the interest of the team as a production unit, such as buying agricultural machinery and improving its irrigation system.

---

[6] For an historical description of the emergence of the people's communes, see, for example, Keith Buchanan, op. cit., pp. 114-142, and Maurice Meisner, op. cit., pp. 140-160, 230-241. For recent reports and discussions on the commune system, see Ward Morehouse, "Notes on Hua-tung Commune," China Quarterly, No. 67 (September 1976), pp. 582-596; Victor D. Lippit, "The Commune in Chinese Development," Modern China, Vol. 3 (April 1977), pp. 229-255; Sartaj Aziz, op. cit., pp. 46-61; and Gordon Bennett, Huadong: The Story of a Chinese Commune (Boulder, Colorado: Westview Press, 1978).

[7] See F. Crook, "The Commune System in the People's Republic of China," in U. S. Congress, Joint Economic Committee, China: A Reassessment of the Economy (Washington, D. C.: Government Printing Office, 1975), p. 375; and Victor D. Lippit, op. cit., p. 232.

[8] For instance, the populations of Huancheng Commune of Xinhui Xian and Dali Commune of Nanhai Xian, both of which the author visited in December 1976, are 59,000 and 68,000, respectively.

The production brigade is the intermediate level above the production team. The brigade coordinates the production plans of its constituent teams according to quotas assigned by the commune as a whole. The brigade also engages in investment and development projects which are too large for the team to handle, such as land reclamation, setting up livestock farms and fruit orchards, and operating small-scale industries (e.g., food processing, paper manufacturing).

The commune, of course, is the level at which major decisions involving the interests of the whole community are made. It is responsible for projects beyond the scope of the brigades, such as water conservancy projects, road construction, and factories for the manufacture of certain agricultural machinery. The commune is also the lowest level of state authority and is thus responsible for implementing national policies in the countryside and serving as the major administrative link between the rural community and the *xian* (county) to which it belongs. Important social services for the whole community such as education and public health are also coordinated at the commune level.

The commune is thus both an agricultural production unit and a unit of local administration combined in such a way that the various aspects of rural development may be better coordinated. The three-level organization just indicated is designed to mobilize manpower and allocate resources to where they are most needed in support of a collectivized economy. Areas of responsibility are fairly well defined while at the same time communication linkages are built into the whole organizational network of the commune to encourage coordination which is necessary if the commune is to perform the various developmental tasks effectively and efficiently. In the process of performing such tasks local initiative is always encouraged to deal with local problems. It can be seen then that administratively this mode of operation requires personnel who are especially committed to the needs and goals of the collectivity and who also share the vision of the role of the commune system in China's national development. Furthermore, the commune development model rests heavily on the establishment of rural industries of various types and scales both to support agriculture and to link the rural sector with the urban sector of industrial development. This means that to a large extent manpower must be trained in the commune in order that rural industrialization may be most readily and efficiently carried out.

Because the commune is usually a huge collectivity, it is not difficult to understand that its functioning depends substantially not so much on its formal organization as on the way in which people work together. The implications for education are clear. Rural education must be geared towards the needs of commune development. Even more important is the necessity for each commune to shape its educational system in accordance with the particular concerns of the commune in question.

CHARACTERISTICS OF COMMUNE EDUCATION

Prior to the Cultural Revolution, rural education was not adequate in quantity or quality to meet rural needs.[9] Full-time regular schools were concentrated in the cities. Age and examination restrictions required for entry to these schools and the expenses involved were highly unfavorable to peasant children. Although a variety of non-regular rural schools, such as the "cultivate-study schools," emerged during the early 1960s, school attendance rates were still quite low.

The important change in rural education policy came in 1969 with the announcement of the "Draft Program of Rural Secondary and Primary Education."[10] That was about one year after Mao Tse-tung made his famous "May 7th Directive" that the length of schooling should be shortened and that education should be revolutionized. The Draft Program called for the running of primary schools by production brigades and secondary schools by communes. It also recommended shortening primary education from six to five years and secondary education from six to four years. Soon this pattern was adopted throughout the country. As a result, the primary schools in the brigades also offer the first two years of secondary education (junior secondary), while the secondary schools operated by the communes are actually two-year senior secondary schools. Of course, this places considerable financial burden on the communes. Very little state subsidy has ever assisted the commune schools. Under the principle of "self-reliance," the commune schools have met their expenses typically through relying on local resources and generating income by operating small farms and small factories which actually serve the production needs of the communes.

In recent years, with the system of commune schools in full operation, popularization of basic education in the rural areas has been greatly enhanced. In most cases, upwards of 90 per cent of primary school age children are able

[9]For a description of the criticisms launched in the Cultural Revolution against the "old" (pre-Cultural Revolution) educational system, see Marianne Bastid, "Economic Necessity and Political Ideals in Educational Reform During the Cultural Revolution," *China Quarterly*, No. 42 (April-June 1970), pp. 16-45.

[10]The "Draft Program" was first published in the *Renmin Ribao* of May 12, 1969. For a commentary on it, see You Xue, "On China's Draft Program for Rural Secondary and Primary Schools," *China Monthly* (Hong Kong), No. 64 (July 1969), pp. 316-319 (in Chinese).

to receive primary education.[11]

What are the main characteristics of the kind of education that the commune schools offer? For our purposes, these characteristics may be described under three interrelated aspects: (1) adaptation of the educational content and teaching methods to agriculture and to the realities of commune life; (2) making the schools directly serve the productional needs of the commune; and (3) encouraging mass participation in commune schools.

1. Adaptation of education to agriculture and to commune life

To ensure that a child's schooling be relevant to his future contribution to the development of the commune system, commune education is shaped according to the needs of the commune. In the curriculum, "agricultural basic knowledge" carries considerable weight, along with the basic subjects of language (both Chinese and English), arithmetic, and politics. Experienced peasants and workers are invited to help with the teaching of certain subjects where necessary. More important, systematic "link-up" (guagou) arrangements have long been established between the schools and their respective brigades or communes to facilitate teaching and learning beyond the confines of the classroom in such a way that the educational value of "outside" resources and facilities is added to school learning. Indeed, the realities of life in the commune generally constitute the "large classroom" and the conventional school classroom is the "small classroom." Students are often taken to visit factories, fields, workshops, and different units in the brigade or the commune to observe various aspects of life and production, and to relate these aspects to what they learn in the school classroom. This they do to implement the principle of "coordination of theory and practice." They may watch experienced peasants at work or workers assembling some farming machinery or listen to elderly villagers telling stories of their past sufferings before the communists came to power. The basic rationale for such activities is simply to help students acquire a first-hand experience of what it means to live and work in a commune and what the "socialist construction" in China is all about.

[11] In Huancheng Commune of Xinhui Xian and Dali Commune of Nanhai Xian, it was reported to the author in December 1976 that over 95 per cent of primary school-age children are able to receive primary education. Of those who finish primary school about 90 per cent will proceed to junior secondary school. Other sources indicate that this tends to be rather typical of other communes in Guangdong province. In the case of the two communes just mentioned, approximately 70 per cent of those who complete junior secondary school will go on to senior secondary school. In Doushan Commune, Taishan Xian and Luogang Commune near the suburban area of Canton, which the author's colleagues visited in May 1978, the proportion of junior secondary school graduates who will proceed to senior secondary school is 50 per cent, and 75 to 80 per cent, respectively.

2. Making schools serve the productional needs of the commune

Just as students are given the opportunity to widen their educational experience beyond the classroom by going out into their surroundings, they are also provided with the chance to familiarize themselves with the tasks and processes of production by working. Commune schools, primary and secondary alike, typically have their own small farms and small factories or workshops where students can learn agricultural and industrial skills. Experienced peasants and workers are invited to assist in setting up these facilities and to provide certain specialized training where needed. These facilities at the primary school level are naturally much simpler than at the secondary school level. The amount of the students' participation in labor is geared to their age. Very young children may simply learn to plant seeds and make toy parts, but the intention is to enable them to adopt a positive attitude toward manual work and to cultivate a concern for the collectivity. At the same time, the work that the students perform is often part of an actual production process. It may be toys or matchboxes in the case of primary schools; it may be mechanical parts or farming tools in the case of secondary schools. Sometimes, a secondary school with adequate equipment and appropriate technical support from the commune may operate a small factory that produces insecticides or chemical fertilizers. Alternatively, a secondary school may have a workshop in which students learn to service and repair certain agricultural machines such as light tractors and water pumps.

In addition to operating small farms and factories/workshops in the schools, it is also quite common for secondary shcools to maintain "link-up" arrangements with nearby brigades and their factories to provide practical training in production. The students spend specified lengths of time in brigade factories or farms learning various technical skills from experienced workers and peasants. Thus, for example, at the Huancheng Secondary School of Huancheng Commune in Guangdong province, the students in the second year of their senior secondary education are divided into four specialization groups all of which spend some time in the brigades learning the skills relevant to their group. The "rural culture" group, for instance, learn propaganda work while the "agricultural machinery" group learn mechanical maintenance and repair. The latter also assist the production teams in such activities as field ploughing and setting up electric wires for lighting in the fields.

To further strengthen the role of education in supporting the developmental tasks of the commune, all schools are expected to participate actively in "scientific experimentation" projects which aim at improving the technological level in agriculture. Through cooperation with agricultural technicians and experimental farms in the communes, many commune schools have mobilized their teachers and students in such endeavors as the development of new wheat and rice breeds, manufacture of agricultural medicines, design of new pest control methods, and improvement of planting systems. Many of the results of these projects have actually been adopted and popularized in production activities.[12]

All the examples cited above point to the fact that not only do students in commune schools learn knowledge and skills directly relevant to production in the communes in ways that combine theory with practice, but they also have numerous opportunities of applying these skills immediately and systematically in their own communities. This being the case, the schools and their educational activities are closely tied with many other functioning parts of the commune. It is, in many ways, a multi-faceted manifestation of Mao Tse-tung's directive that education should be combined with productive labor.

3. Mass participation in commune schools

That the education offered by commune schools is oriented toward local needs is largely the result of placing rural education completely in the control of the communes, and the general policy of encouraging mass participation in educational matters following the Cultural Revolution. The basic rationale is that since education is to serve the needs of the masses, the latter ought to play a substantial part in the shaping and implementation of education. Since the late 1960s, school management has been in the hands of school revolutionary committees, the membership of which includes representatives of peasants and local militia units. Funds for running the schools come from the production brigades (primary schools) and the communes (secondary schools), as many of the teachers are paid on the basis of workpoints like other commune members, and incomes are generated from products and services of the schools' small farms and factories. The planning and implementation of educational matters have become an integral part of the responsibility and leadership of the production brigades and the communes generally, so that each brigade or commune is able to influence and shape local education directly in accordance with local conditions.

IMPLICATIONS FOR RURAL DEVELOPMENT

Having briefly described the major characteristics of commune education, we must now ask the important question, "What implications does China's

---

[12]*Guangming Ribao* [Bright Daily], "Intensively Criticize Lin Biao and Confucius, and Insist on Open-door Education" (April 22, 1974); and "To Teach for the Revolution Is Merit; To Learn for the Revolution Is Glory" (February 28, 1977).

commune education have for its rural development?" It will not be possible to answer this question exhaustively here, but an attempt is made to highlight certain main points. In doing so we need to keep in mind China's task of rural development, outlined earlier, as well as the Chinese concept of development which cannot be stated simply in economic and material terms, since it connotes a system of human values and socialist aims.[13]

(1) By building a school system within each commune, with the size of the system geared to the population of the commune, the task of expansion of education and universalization of basic education among the huge rural masses of China is made much easier. Inasmuch as a basic level of literacy and educational attainment is fundamental to any substantial social and economic development, the existence of commune schools has a definite instrumental value.

(2) Since the planning and organization of the commune school system is basically the responsibility of the commune and its constituent production brigades, education may be related more closely to local production needs and manpower requirements. Just as the commune itself is a fairly autonomous unit of local administration, so educational matters are in large measure subject to decentralized management. Education is thus made more responsive to local conditions in the rural areas. Furthermore, the viability of the commune as a model of development is strengthened because education is actively engaged in promoting commune goals.

(3) By adapting the content and methods of education to the realities and needs of production in the commune, education is made highly relevant to the development of the commune. Not only can children and youths acquire a practical training that provides them with a clear notion of their potential contribution to the commune, the commune is also assured of maintaining and developing a pool of suitably-trained manpower on which the future of the commune can depend. There have been numerous reports indicating the preponderance of locally educated technicians, peasants, workers, administrators, and other personnel in the communes. Some of these may have received further training at higher level institutions in urban areas but have returned to serve the commune they come from. Of course, there are also technical and administrative personnel despatched from other areas or trained elsewhere,

[13]The centrality of values and moral incentives in the Chinese conception of development is discussed at length in E. L. Wheelwright and Bruce McFarlane, *The Chinese Road to Socialism* (Harmondsworth: Penguin Books, 1970), pp. 147-163, and in Derek Bryan, "Changing Social Ethics in Contemporary China," in William A. Robson and Bernard Crick (eds.), *China in Transition* (Beverly Hills: Sage Publications, 1975), pp. 53-61. See also A. Doak Barnett, *op. cit.*, p. 13, and Peter Worsley, *Inside China* (London: Allen Lane, 1975), p. 202.

but the fact that the communes themselves are capable of training a considerable proportion of the manpower they need, especially that at an intermediate level, greatly strengthens their potential for development.[14]

(4) As indicated earlier, one important task of rural development in China is the establishment of a variety of rural industries to support the development of agriculture. These industries capitalize on local resources, stimulate the development and diffusion of indigenous technology that can serve local needs, and provide considerable employment opportunities for the rural population. The supply of technical manpower to serve in these rural industries (e.g., fertilizers, farming machinery, facilities for machinery repair, light consumer goods, food processing, etc.) and the growth of these industries are facilitated by the practical orientation of commune education. As already mentioned, the schools make provision for training their students in various agricultural and industrial skills, and are also keen to contribute to technological improvement through various "scientific experimentation" programs.

(5) In addition to transmitting useful knowledge and skills, the commune schools are highly instrumental in socializing the young toward an understanding and acceptance of an ideology which stresses the overarching importance of the collectivity. Throughout the schooling years, the students are constantly taught, both in theory and in practice, the meaning and necessity of "serving the people" and the spirit of "self-reliance." In fact, the bulk of the commune schools themselves have been set up according to these cardinal principles. The learning experience obtained from the "large classroom" (the community) and from participating in productive labor serves to widen their horizon so as to be concerned with the interests of the larger collectivity. Furthermore, it also serves to develop in them a positive attitude toward manual work. The latter is highly important since education in many developing countries has too often produced an intellectual elite who aspire only to white collar and managerial jobs and who would hardly want to serve in the countryside. With such a vast countryside and a huge rural population, China cannot afford to have such an intellectual elite. This was precisely part of Mao Tse-tung's intention when he called for a thorough reform in education during the Cultural Revolution. Mao wanted China to become an egalitarian society in which not only is there an equitable distribution of wealth (through a collectivized economy) but one in which the barriers that separate people from each other would be removed.[15] One such barrier which is characteristic

[14] Aziz, op. cit., p. 55.

[15] A perceptive analysis of Maoist educational values with reference to egalitarianism is Donald J. Munro's "Egalitarian Ideal and Educational Fact in Communist China," in John M. H. Lindbeck (ed.), China: Management of a Revolutionary Society (Seattle: University of Washington Press, 1971), pp. 256-301.

of traditional Chinese society is that between those who "work with their minds" (intellectuals and administrators) and those who "work with their hands" (peasants and workers).

Where such a barrier exists it is difficult to implement rural developmental projects in accordance with such principles as "self-reliance" and "serving the people," since these principles call for a deep commitment to collective causes. Although that barrier has not been totally eliminated, it would still be accurate to say that in China to-day people are well accustomed to appreciating the importance of productive labor, be it in the factories or in the fields. Education may be said to be largely responsible for bringing this about.

(6) Finally, since the commune schools are typically outreaching in their educational endeavors, their students and teachers are expected to be highly concerned with the welfare of the commune and its constituent parts (brigades and teams). In the course of carrying out teaching and learning activities, they may engage in various kinds of community service work, such as offering technical assistance in irrigation projects, developing better feeds for livestock, and planting experimental fields in cooperation with commune members.[16]

In this way, not only is the value of "serving the people" reinforced, but also the students and teachers become highly aware of the various needs of the commune. The new generation thus trained have not only the skills but, in addition, the commitment and willingness to serve their own community. Their satisfaction lies in helping the countryside prosper. Insofar as this quality is indeed achieved in its manpower, there is substantial hope for rural development.

DISCUSSION AND CONCLUSION

The spread of education is itself part of the development process since the provision of education, like that of health and other welfare services, is necessary to meet the basic social needs of a population. But this is mainly the consumption aspect of education. In addition, education may be viewed as investment in human capital with the hope that the product of education will have a useful input into the development process. This perspective is generally taken in the developing countries, and usually advocated by writers on development.[17] What is likely to be problematic, however, is the linkage

[16] See, for example, Guangming Ribao, "To Teach for the Revolution Is Merit; To Learn for the Revolution Is Glory" (February 28, 1977), and Hong Qi [Red Flag], "Open-door Education is Getting More and More Impressive," No. 12 (1975), pp. 40-43.

[17] See, John K. Galbraith, Economic Development in Perspective (New York: Fawcett Publications, 1962), pp. 60-76; Theodore W. Schultz, The Economic Value of Education (New York: Columbia University Press, 1963), pp. 38-46; Adam Curle, Educational

between education and other spheres of development. Is education designed in such a way as to meet local manpower needs? Is the education that the young receive such that they are suitably equipped and committed to work for rural development? Does education contribute to a diversification of the rural economy? Is education capable of instilling in the young the ideology on which the whole social structure of the society rests? These are among the major questions particularly relevant to China's rural development.

We have pointed out that primary and secondary education for the rural population in China is organized and operated by the communes which are by now well-established bodies of rural local administration as well as units of large-scale collectivized production. We have also described the ways in which this commune-run educational system is oriented toward local needs and adapted to agricultural requirements. This has been made possible by the implementation of a policy which stresses the following: (1) the development of human resources not only in pure manpower requirement terms, but also in terms of value commitment, as required for building a socialist country; (2) the importance of integrating education with local administration, production activities and rural life in general, in order to maximize education's relevance and utility in rural development; and (3) the need to use education as a means to strengthen the commitment of not just the leaders and administrators but also the rural masses to the commune system and the many tasks of "socialist construction" for the sake of a more egalitarian society. To appreciate the significance of these policy emphases more fully, let us dwell on their meaning a little longer.

First, it must be remembered that China's development objective is basically to become a modern socialist country by the end of the present century. In many ways, this requires not just technology and the boosting of economic growth but also the commitment to a set of socialist values. From the Chinese point of view, such values call for both an orientation to collective needs as a primary action goal as well as the principle of "walking on two legs" as a strategy to achieve that goal. Thus, "to serve the people" is the action goal; and "self-reliance," which is directly relevant to development of rural potentials and is an application of the "walking on two legs" principle, becomes a development strategy. Although China is now much more outreaching in international relations compared to a few years ago, and has embarked on a number of projects to absorb Western experience to facilitate its own economic and technological growth, this can be seen as basically a more extensive

---

Strategy for Developing Societies, 2nd edition (London: Tavistock Publications, 1970), pp. 140-142; and Christopher Howe, *China's Economy: A Basic Guide* (London: Paul Elek, 1978), pp. 21-22.

application of the "two legs" principle, without any substantive change in the core of China's socialist values. As has been observed by many writers on Chinese development, the combination of modernization efforts and commitment to socialist values is China's unique quality as a development model.[18] The viability of this model therefore hinges greatly on the degree to which education can cultivate and strengthen value commitment at the same time as it is training manpower.

Secondly, given the centrality of socialist value commitment, education must seek ways and means to demonstrate the rationale of such values. If the content and methods of education are integrated with the realities and needs of the commune, the viability of the commune model and the values which this model represents are more effectively demonstrated.

Finally—and this is closely related to the above two points—assuming that commune education does indeed serve the instrumental purpose of cultivating a socialist value commitment, the responsibility for supporting and facilitating the future of the commune system and hence rural development generally falls in effect on the shoulders of the commune masses themselves. This is especially so with the accumulation of the results of rural industrialization and diversification of rural economic activities.

Allowing for the existence of regional differences—some of which are still quite marked—many rural communes have increased their productivity as well as their employment opportunities and have thus improved their quality of life over the years. This being the case, differences between rural and urban areas have been greatly reduced. To a large extent, this has been possible not only because China has chosen the commune model of development but also because a very important aspect of China's socialist value system is to strive toward a more egalitarian society. China makes no pretense that egalitarianism has been achieved already. However, as far as inequalities arising from barriers between mental and manual work, and barriers between town and country are concerned, one has to admit that a considerable social transformation has indeed taken place. By adapting rural education to commune needs, by making education a community concern, and by stressing the importance of commitment to socialist values, it seems fair to say that the Chinese have expended considerable efforts in allocating a primary role to education as an integral part of rural development. As China has recently decided to move more rapidly towards a modern economy, more attention will have to be paid to the quality of education in terms of technical skills and academic standards. The whole

[18] See, Michael Gasster, *China's Struggle to Modernize* (New York: Alfred A. Knopf, 1972), pp. 97-141; John G. Gurley, *China's Economy and the Maoist Strategy* (New York: Monthly Review Press, 1976), pp. 256-257; and Alexander Eckstein, *op. cit.*, pp. 277-285.

66   Building China: Studies in Integrated Development

educational system will need to be further expanded, while becoming much
more selective and competitive than previously. In rural education, it may
well be that in the process the effort towards achieving more egalitarianism
through a socialist value commitment may be affected. But such developments
are still in the future.

CHAPTER FOUR
The Development of Rural Health Care*

Rance P. L. Lee and Wai-ying Tsui

Political stability and economic growth are important aspirations of most developing countries today, but so is the modernization of health care services. Essentially, health care modernization means the delivery of the best medical care to the greatest number of people in the country. It requires not only an upgrading of the technical quality of medical work but also a reform in the organizational aspect of the health care delivery system.

Health workers in most developing countries face a common problem: the great majority of the population live in the mass rural areas but most, and also the best, medical care services are concentrated in a few urban centers. The distribution of health services thus favors the relatively rich and relatively skilled urban minority at the expense of the relatively poor and unskilled rural majority.[1] The problem becomes more serious if we take into consideration the fact that the rural masses are particularly exposed and particularly prone to a wide variety of diseases. To modernize the health care system, therefore, it is necessary to overcome the disparity between rural and urban sectors. In other words, health workers should walk to the countryside, instead of standing still in the urban centers. The question is: How do they walk from cities to villages?

*The present study was supported by a grant from the Board of Trustees of Lingnan University. It is part of the "Commune and Socio-economic Development in Communist China" research program sponsored by the Social Research Centre of The Chinese University of Hong Kong. The research program was directed by Mr. S. L. Wong in 1976-77, and is presently directed by Dr. Rance P. L. Lee. The authors wish to acknowledge the advice and support of Professor C. K. Yang, and the assistance of Miss Helen Siu, Miss Har-bing Wong, Miss Man-tsun Cheng, and Dr. Robert Dan.
[1] Susan B. Rifkin and Raphael Kaplinsky, "Health Strategy and Development Planning: Lessons from the People's Republic of China," *Journal of Development Studies*, Vol. 9 (January 1973), pp. 213-232.

Different countries may have different answers to this question.[2] In this chapter let us look into some of the ways in which the People's Republic of China has attempted to modernize the system of health care delivery to the rural masses. In particular, we shall use empirical data to demonstrate that (1) both Chinese and Western medical care are introduced to the rural regions, and (2) the two systems of medical care operate in a coordinated, rather than competing, manner. An examination of China's rural health care strategies is important, as China seems to be rather successful in meeting health needs in rural areas.[3]

RURAL ORGANIZATION IN CHINA

It is estimated that there are roughly 900 million people in China, of which about 80 per cent are rural dwellers. Since 1958, the people's commune has been the basic unit for the organization of social life and for the utilization of manpower in rural areas.[4] There are currently some 50,000 people's communes in rural China.[5]

The commune is a highly integrated multi-functional system. It functions as a relatively self-contained unit integrating all the essential aspects of community life such as farming, industry, commerce, school education, welfare, health care, recreation, public works, and public security. The commune has its own government and all the resources are collectively owned by members

[2] See V. Djukanovic and E. P. March (eds.), *Alternative Approaches to Meeting Basic Health Needs in Developing Countries* (Geneva: World Health Organization, 1975).

[3] See R. M. Worth, "Strategy of Change in the People's Republic of China—The Rural Health Center," in D. Lerner and W. Schramm (eds.), *Communication and Change in the Developing Countries* (Honolulu: East-West Center Books, 1967), pp. 217-230; T. H. Cheng, "Disease Control and Prevention in China," *Asia* (New York), Vol. 26 (1972), pp. 31-59; V. W. Sidel and R. Sidel, *Serve the People: Observations on Medicine in the People's Republic of China* (Boston: Beacon Press, 1973); and P. Wilenski, *The Delivery of Health Services in the People's Republic of China* (Canada: International Development Research Center, 1976).

[4] For a discussion on China's rural organization before the commune system, see Kung-chuan Hsiao, *Rural China: Imperial Control in the Nineteenth Century* (Seattle & London: University of Washington Press, 1960); Hsiao-t'ung Fei, *Peasant Life in China* (London: Kegan Paul, 1939); Sidney D. Gamble, *Ting Hsien: A North China Rural Community* (Stanford: Stanford University Press, 1954); C. K. Yang, *A Chinese Village in Early Communist Transition* (Cambridge, Mass.: M.I.T. Press, 1959); and Keith Buchanan, *The Transformation of the Chinese Earth: Perspectives on Modern China* (London: G. Bell & Sons, 1970), Chapter 6. Hsiao deals with rural China in the nineteenth century. Fei and Gamble report on the rural organizations in some villages in the early twentieth century. Yang and Buchanan describe the changes in village life shortly before and after the Communist revolution.

[5] *Tai-kung pao*, January 31, 1978. (A Chinese newspaper published in Hong Kong.)

of the commune. Structurally, each commune is typically subdivided into several production brigades, while each brigade consists of a certain number of production teams. It is through the commune organization that the health care services are developed and delivered to the rural masses in China. In each commune, there are normally one commune health clinic and some branch clinics at the commune level, one medical station in each production brigade, and one to two health aids in each production team. In the following pages, we shall use some of the data from one of the rural communes we visited in recent years, for the purpose of illustrating health care development in rural China.

The commune is called Huancheng, which is part of the Xinhui County of the Guangdong Province.[6] It is situated in the vicinity of the county capital and is about 75 kilometers southwest of Guangzhou (Canton), the capital city of Guangdong. We visited the commune on three occasions: December 1976, May 1978, and December 1978. We had a number of individual meetings with health workers, cadres and peasants, and visited several health units in the commune.

At the end of 1978, the Huancheng Commune had nearly 60,000 members living in a total area of 68 square kilometers. The population density is 882 persons per square kilometer. The commune is administratively subdivided into 29 production brigades and 190 production teams. On the average, there are 1,851 persons in each brigade and 283 persons in each production team. The administrative headquarters is situated in the commune's market town.

Huancheng has one market town, located in the neighborhood of the capital town of Xinhui County. Most people are engaged in agricultural activities. About 89.5 per cent of the total population are classified as agricultural population, 2.5 per cent as industrial workers, and 8 per cent as town residents. A total area of 4,580 hectares has been cultivated. Rice is the leading crop, followed by palm leaves, sugarcane, peanuts, fruits and vegetables. In addition to the agricultural production by production teams, the commune has established nine industrial undertakings (paper-making, food-processing, sun-drying of palm leaves, machinery repair, transportation, construction, and the manufacturing of palm-leaf products, farm tools, and bricks) and five agricultural enterprises (fish ponds, livestock and poultry, forest products, scientific research, and fruits).

---

[6] The Xinhui County presently has 20 people's communes. According to the *Guangzhou (Canton) Evening News* on 18th April, 1966, the Guangdong Province had a total of more than 1,600 communes.

CHINESE AND WESTERN HEALTH CARE

In the Huancheng Commune, we found that the two types of medical care —Western and Chinese—coexisted. As of December 1978, there were a total of seven professional doctors, of whom two were Chinese-style and five were Western-style practitioners. In addition, there were 16 Chinese-style and 15 Western-style assistant doctors. The professional doctors were graduates from a five-year course at the university level or with equivalent experience, while the assistant doctors were graduates from a three-year course at the secondary level. Taking both professional and assistant doctors together, the doctor to population ratio in the commune was about 1 to 1,580.

Both Chinese-style and Western-style doctors are available for consultation by the people, and it is up to the patients to choose between the two types of doctors.

Efforts have been made to integrate the Chinese and Western methods. In Huancheng, both Chinese-style and Western-style doctors have been given opportunities to learn not only their own medical tradition but also some basic concepts and skills in the other approach. These opportunities include, for instance, medical school training, and some short-term special sessions organized by commune or the county. We were told that it is not unusual for a doctor to use both Chinese and Western methods for diagnosis and treatment, and that some patients are attended jointly by the Chinese-style and the Western-style doctors.

The Chinese-style and the Western-style doctors in the commune are the same in terms of prestige and reward. The professional doctors of both traditions are classified as senior-grade staff, while the assistant doctors are classified as intermediate-grade staff. Moreover, doctors of the same grade have the same salary scale, regardless of the medical traditions. On the average, the monthly salary is about US$40 for professional doctors and about US$33 for assistant doctors.

The doctors in Huancheng are assisted by a number of supporting staff. There are 34 nurses, 3 dentists, 3 midwives, 2 Chinese-style medical apprentices, and 13 nursing and technical assistants. We learned that these medical staff are mainly in the Western medical tradition, but they have been trained with some basic skills in Chinese medicine. The nurses, dentists and midwives are classified as intermediate-grade staff being paid, on the average, about US$33 a month. The nursing and technical assistants are junior-grade staff receiving, on the average, a monthly salary of about US$27.

The barefoot-doctor scheme was introduced into Huancheng in 1967. As of December 1978, the commune had a total of 90 barefoot doctors. The Health Bureau at the provincial level had set a standard for the commune that there should be one barefoot doctor for every 500 persons, and that if a medical station had more than one barefoot doctor, then at least one of them should be a female. These standards apply to all the communes within the Guangdong Province.

Initially the commune's barefoot doctors were trained for one year, of which six months were for course work and six months for clinical practice. After some years of service they then attended a formal course, ranging from three to six months, for further training on a comprehensive basis. Sixty-six per cent of the barefoot doctors in Huancheng have already received such further training. Moreover, since May 1978 they have also participated in the one-year correspondence course of more advanced training. The correspondence course is organized by the County Health Bureau at the request of the Provincial Health Bureau. It is expected that by the year 1980, all barefoot doctors will achieve the same standard as the assistant doctors.

In addition to the initial and further training on a comprehensive basis, barefoot doctors are also required to attend some short-term sessions dealing with specific topics such as the use of certain contraceptives, and the prevention and treatment of a particular disease. Another measure to upgrade the quality of barefoot doctors is regular meetings among barefoot doctors. Under the supervision of professional doctors, the barefoot doctors from various regions of the commune meet together once a month for the purpose of reporting new cases or methods, and exchanging views and experiences.

As a result of the various learning opportunities, the barefoot doctors are equipped with a variety of both Chinese and Western medical knowledge.[7] They are capable of dealing with some ordinary and relatively minor diseases such as flu and colds, upper respiratory tract infections, furuncles and carbuncles, indigestion, parasitic diseases, and minor sprains and injuries. Visiting some barefoot-doctor offices, we found a number of medical instruments, medicinal materials, instructional manuals and periodicals (e.g., *New Chinese Medicine*, *New Medicine*, and the *Journal of Barefoot Doctors*) in both Chinese and Western medical traditions.

We were informed that the total number of outpatient consultations in the commune is about 1,200 a day, of which about 60 to 70 per cent are attended by barefoot doctors. Apparently, the barefoot doctors have played an important role in the commune's health care system. It should be emphasized that the barefoot doctors perform multiple functions. In addition to the treatment of common illnesses, they are also responsible for preventive services

[7] See, for instance, P.K.M. New and M. L. New, "Health Care in the People's Republic of China: The Barefoot Doctor," *Inquiry*, Vol. 12 (Supplement 1975), pp. 103-113; and *A Barefoot Doctor's Manual*, The American Translation of the Official Chinese Paramedical Manual (Philadelphia: Running Press, 1977).

and health education. Planned fertility, obstetrics and gynecology are also the responsibility of female barefoot doctors.

Apart from barefoot doctors, the commune has a total of 380 health aids working in the various production teams. They are recruited from among peasants, and are engaged in farming most of the time. Most of them were trained by barefoot doctors for one week every year. After learning some simple skills in Chinese and Western medicine, they serve as first aids to members of their own production teams. Sometimes they also assist the barefoot doctors in immunization services, environmental sanitation, and nursing care.

In summary, the Huancheng commune as a whole has a total of 563 medical and health workers, including 2 Chinese-style and 5 Western-style professional doctors, 16 Chinese-style and 15 Western-style assistant doctors, 3 dentists, 3 midwives, 2 Chinese-style medical apprentices, 34 nurses, 13 nursing and technical assistants, 90 barefoot doctors, and 380 health aids. These workers provide both Chinese and Western medical care services to a total of nearly 60,000 people over an area of 68 square kilometers. It was reported that of all the medicines prescribed by the commune's health workers, about 50 per cent are Chinese and the other 50 per cent are Western.

COORDINATION OF THE TWO SYSTEMS

Both Chinese and Western medical care services in rural areas have been organized into a unified health network. The organizational structure is essentially a form of regionalization.

Ever since the beginning of this century, the concept of regionalization has been widely discussed. Fundamentally, the concept implies that the region be divided into well-defined geographical areas, each of which has a population large enough to allow the provision of comprehensive services in an economic way, and that the various services be arranged in a graded hierarchy with a two-way flow of patients, information, personnel, and technology, etc. From an organizational point of view, the health service system in China's rural communes can be conceived as a regionalized network. There are health units at the commune, brigade, and production team levels, forming a graded heirarchy of services with different levels of responsibility and different degrees of technical competency. This three-level health network provides a comprehensive range of Chinese and Western health services, including the prevention and treatment of diseases, health education, scientific research and planned fertility.

1. At the commune level

Huancheng has one commune health clinic and five branch clinics. The commune health clinic serves as the center of the commune's regionalized health care system. It is situated at the market town of the commune, and is equipped with the best facilities and the most qualified health manpower of the commune. It provides both Chinese and Western medical care, and both outpatient and inpatient services.

The commune health clinic is staffed by 1 Chinese-style and 5 Western-style professional doctors, 11 Chinese-style and 7 Western-style assistant doctors, 2 dentists, 28 nurses, 13 nursing and technical assistants, 3 midwives and 17 administrative staff. The outpatient services are provided by both the Chinese and Western sections of the clinic. The Chinese section consists of Departments of Medicine, Surgery, Orthopedics, Dermatology, and Palpation and Massage Therapy, while the Western section consists of Departments of Medicine, Surgery, Dentistry, and Eye, Ear, Nose & Throat. On the average, there are about 500 outpatient visits a day. In addition to the various outpatient departments, the clinic has organized two special units: one for prevention and immunization, and another for maternal and child care and fertility control.

Regarding inpatient care, there is a surgical ward for men and another for women, a medical ward for men and another for women, and an insulating room for patients with infectious diseases. There are 53 beds. There is an operating room equipped with oxygen, simple surgical tools, and shadowless lamps. The doctors are capable of doing abdominal operations (mostly on appendicitis, stomach and gall-bladder) and sterilization. The patients are referred to the county hospital for more complicated operations such as those on chest and brain.

The commune health clinic has two X-ray machines and one ultra-short-wave machine. There is also a medical laboratory, an ambulance, and a pharmacy with several hundred items of Chinese and Western medicinal materials. The clinic has a pharmaceutical factory capable of making a few items of Western medicines (e.g., glucose and saline water) and some 60 items of Chinese patent medicines. We were informed that about 30 per cent of the medicines consumed by the commune are self-manufactured.

The clinic's five branch clinics are located in the densely populated and relatively remote areas of the commune. They provide mainly outpatient services, although there may be a few inpatient beds. The Dongjia Branch Clinic has one Chinese-style and one Western-style assistant doctor, and one nurse. The Mei Jiang Branch Clinic has one Chinese-style professional doctor and one Chinese-style medical apprentice. The Tianma Branch Clinic has three Chinese-style and five Western-style assistant doctors, one dentist, three nurses, and one administrative staff. The Chakeng Branch Clinic has one Chinese-style assistant doctor, one Chinese-style medical apprentice, one Western-style assistant doctor, and one nurse. The Jiulong Branch Clinic has one Western-style assistant doctor and one nurse.

Apart from the commune health clinic and branch clinics, the commune has established five medical stations, one for each of the commune's agricultural or industrial enterprises with over one hundred workers. These medical stations are staffed by barefoot doctors. They are responsible for the prevention of occupational diseases and for the outpatient care of the employees.

2. At the brigade level

Each production brigade of the Huancheng Commune has set up one medical station, except the Chakeng Brigade which has two medical stations.[8] As the commune consists of 29 brigades, there are altogether 30 brigade medical stations. Each brigade medical station is staffed, on the average, by two to three barefoot doctors, responsible for the prevention and treatment of some common and relatively minor illnesses of the brigade members. No inpatient care is provided.

In each brigade medical station, there are some Western facilities (e.g., theremometers, stethoscopes, sphygmomanometer, and injectors) as well as Chinese medical equipment (e.g., acupuncture needles and maps of acupuncture points). There is a dispensary with a number of commonly-used patent medicines. Seven of the 30 brigade medical stations have also set up a special dispensary for Chinese herbs.

One industrial unit of the Tianma Brigade employs over one hundred workers, and for this reason has set up a medical station of its own.

3. At the production team level

Each production team has assigned two members to serve as health aids, providing primarily first aid services. They are agricultural workers who perform health duties only when needed. The health aids of each production team are equipped with a medical box with some simple instruments and first aid medicines.

We have shown that the Huancheng Commune has a variety of health units at different levels. The commune health clinic and its five branch clinics are the central units of the commune's health care system. The 36 medical stations (5 for the commune's enterprises, 30 for production brigades, and 1 for a brigade's enterprise) are staffed by barefoot doctors, serving as intermediate units of the health care system. The two health aids in each production team are the local units. As the commune has 190 production teams, there are 380 health aids spreading out in the various regions of the commune. In effect, the commune has a three-level network of regionalized health care services.

[8] Because the Chakeng Brigade's villages are scattered and are severed by a hill.

Administratively, the health units are owned and managed by the cadres and the people at the corresponding levels. However, the health aids of production teams are supervised by barefoot doctors of brigade medical stations, who are in turn supervised by professional and assistant doctors of the communes health clinic. The branch clinics and the medical stations for industrial or agricultural enterprises are also supervised by the commune health clinic.

There is a constant flow of patient and health resources between the three levels of health units. Patients may be referred by the health aids to the brigade medical station, and may then be referred to the commune health clinic. Patients discharged from the commune health clinic may be sent home, and then looked after by barefoot doctors or health aids. Periodically, barefoot doctors of a brigade medical station offer short-term training sessions for health aids of the brigade's production teams, while the commune health clinic organizes training opportunities for barefoot doctors of the various brigades. Should there be a discovery of new cases or methods, the information would flow both vertically and horizontally through the issuing of circulars or by periodic conferences and meetings. In the case of conducting health education or prevention campaigns, the commune health clinic would mobilize barefoot doctors, who then work with health aids in mobilizing the masses.

It should be pointed out that the commune's health care system is not self-contained. It is linked to, and thus supported by, health units at the county level. Difficult cases, for instance, may be referred to the county's health units for treatment. It was reported that about 20 per cent of the cases are so referred. In other words, the commune's health care system can deal with about 80 per cent of the cases.

The Xinhui County, of which Huancheng is a part, has a people's hospital (providing mainly Western medical care), a Chinese medical hospital, a school for training health manpower, a maternal and child care center, a station for prevention and treatment of chronic illnesses, and a prevention and immunization station. These health units at the county level are coordinated by the county's Health Bureau. Besides serving the residents in the capital town of the county, they (1) provide a higher level of outpatient and inpatient care to those patients referred by the county's commune health clinics; (2) disseminate health information and distribute medical supplies to the various communes; (3) offer both initial and further training opportunities for health workers in the communes; and (4) mobilize and coordinate the various communes in the conduct of mass health campaigns or epidemiological surveys.

In between the county level and the commune level is the "regional health clinic." The Xinhui County has 20 communes. As each commune has one commune health clinic, there are 20 commune health clinics in the county. Five commune health clinics have been assigned by the county as regional health clinics. Their major function is to coordinate and support the health clinics of neighboring communes. They are usually better staffed and equipped than other commune health clinics. Recently, Huancheng's commune health clinic has been assigned as the sixth regional health clinic in the Xinhui County. The clinic is thus undertaking various projects to advance its facilities and manpower. For example, the inpatient ward is being expanded and the number of beds will increase from 53 to 100.

The health service network of the county as a whole is not a closed system either. The health units at the county (Xinhui) level are linked to those at the prefectural (Foshan) level, and then to those at the provincial (Guangdong) level. Therefore, should we focus on a province, the regionalized health network would consist of health services ranging from the provincial and the prefectural, through the county and the "regional," down to the commune, the brigade, and the production team levels. In general, the higher the level, the better is the quality and the greater is the quantity of health services. Because of such a regionalized network, a great variety of both Chinese and Western health services can be delivered to the rural masses in China.

We have discussed the development of a regionalized system of Chinese and Western medical care in the commune. It should be recognized that the regionalization process has been facilitated by at least two essential features of the health care system itself. They are the emphasis on prevention and the establishment of a cooperative medical scheme.

Prevention has been taken as a priority in China's rural health programs. In Huancheng, the commune health clinic has organized a special unit for prevention and immunization services. The unit is led by a professional doctor who is in charge of planning and executing preventive programs in the commune. The treatment of common diseases and the provision of first aid services are important duties of the barefoot doctors and health aids, but so are preventive measures. With the assistance of health aids, the barefoot doctors are also responsible for providing immunization services, conducting health propaganda and campaigns, and promoting environmental sanitation. Most commune members, especially the children, have been immunized against a number of diseases such as tuberculosis, B encephalitis, cholera, measles, smallpox, diphtheria, pertussis, tetanus, infantile paralysis, and leptospirosis. Western-style immunizations are generally accepted by the people, but herbal teas are also used for strengthening the organs of the body and for preventing some common diseases such as indigestion, anaemia, respiratory tract infections, flus and colds.

Regarding health propaganda, we saw a number of health educational posters on the bulletin boards in various places of the commune. Moreover, the so-called "patriotic public health campaigns" are carried out four times a year. In the campaigns the rural masses are mobilized by health workers to clean the environment by measures such as the maintenance of water and food hygiene, the elimination of mosquitos, flies and rats, and the control of human and animal waste.

Another important feature of the commune's health care system was the introduction of the cooperative medical scheme in 1968. In Huancheng, each member contributes about US$1.50 a year while his production team contributes about US$3.60 a year for each member. He is then entitled to get free medical care, apart from paying a very small registration fee. The contributions from the commune members and production teams are pooled and used for subsidizing the medical care expenses, such as purchasing medicines and supplies, and paying for medical consultations outside the commune.

The emphasis on prevention has helped cut down the morbidity rates and thus the demand for curative care, while the introduction of the cooperative medical scheme has helped finance the health services. As a result, a regionalized health care system can be successful although the commune itself has scarce economic resources.

CONCLUSION

Delivery of health services to the rural masses is a common concern among many developing countries. From our field trips to the Huancheng Commune in the southern part of China, we found that the People's Republic of China has been providing medical services in a coordinated manner. A wide range of both Chinese and Western medical services are not only available for use by the commune members, but also organized into a regionalized three-level health care network. There is a commune health clinic and branch clinics at the commune level, medical stations at the brigade level, and health aids at the production team level. There are also medical stations for the relatively large industrial or agricultural enterprises in the commune. The commune health clinic and branch clinics are staffed by both Chinese-style and Western-style doctors, while the medical stations are staffed by barefoot doctors who have been trained in some basic skills in both Chinese and Western medicine. There is a constant flow of patients and health resources between the health units at the different levels. It should be recognized that the development of the commune's health network has been strengthened by some essential features of the health care system itself, such as the emphasis on prevention and the establishment of the cooperative medical scheme.

Different countries may have different socio-economic and health conditions. China's model of rural health care may not be entirely applicable to other countries. But the idea of encouraging and coordinating different medical systems deserves some careful consideration. Western medical science is good, but other medical traditions should not be rejected outright. Attempts should be made to make use of them, to coordinate them with Western medical services.

CHAPTER FIVE

Mass Mobilization for Development: Water Conservancy in China*

Ying-keung Chan

"Let agriculture be the foundation, and industry the leading factor" is China's general policy for the development of her national economy. However, to build the foundation and ensure all-round development China has to rely heavily on the improvement of production conditions. Water conservancy, usually regarded as the lifeline of agriculture, is one of the most important prerequisites. Observing from a distance, we get the general impression that China has successfully developed many water conservancy schemes in the past two decades. But what is the real picture?

In the 1950s, development in water conservancy, which had long been urgently needed in China, was marked by the scarcity of capital, machinery, materials, technical experts, but abundance of manpower. Making full use of the available resources, particularly manpower, was the only way to carry out construction widely and efficiently. The slogan "the masses, when organized and united together, and equipped with pooled local resources, are capable of great construction" indicated a belief in transforming population size, very often regarded as a limiting factor, into a facilitating factor in the course of development.

As a general policy, construction for water conservancy in China was mainly small-scale, with medium-scale projects as supplements. However, large-scale

*The present study was supported by a grant from the Board of Trustees of Lingnan University. It is part of the "Commune and Socio-economic Development in Communist China" research sponsored by the Social Research Centre of The Chinese University of Hong Kong. The research program was directed by Mr. S. L. Wong in 1976-77, and is presently directed by Dr. Rance P. L. Lee. During the first field trip taken in December 1976, two communes in Guangdong Province were visited intensively, namely, Huancheng Commune of Xinhui County and Dali Commune of Nanhai County. In the second field trip taken in May 1978, the research team visited these two communes again and also two other communes: Doushan Commune of Taishan County and Luogang Commune in the suburban area of Canton. This chapter has used mainly the data collected in the above mentioned field trips.

ones were also carried out, provided conditions were appropriate and demands for them urgent. Usually, when developing new projects of multi-purpose capability, existing facilities and installations were also strengthened.[1] The rationale was that to commence with large-scale, centrally-run schemes requiring high levels of concentration and utilization of various scarce resources would be unrealistic. It was much easier to concentrate the limited resources on small-scale projects, achieving results in the shortest possible time. Small-scale local projects, when linked into a system, could be expected to function like large-scale ones. Thus the development of small- or medium-scale local projects seemed to offer a sensible solution from the beginning. However, there remains the basic question: Under what organizational framework and how, can the resources for construction be acquired, the manpower potential be fully developed and rationally utilized, in order to achieve the developmental goal? This chapter, with special reference to examples in Guangdong Province, will examine how construction of various scales was achieved.

THE PEOPLE'S COMMUNE AS THE BASIC UNIT

Under the general policy of starting with small-scale projects, the basic administrative unit in the rural sector—the People's Commune—becomes the basic unit in water conservancy. The reason is that the establishment of the People's Commune in the rural sector in the late 1950s provided not only an organizational framework, but also created favorable conditions for the realization of much construction.

First, the "sufficiently large" size, in terms of population and area,[2] and the "higher degree of collective ownership" of the commune facilitates the comprehensive planning of projects within its boundaries and permits the concentrating of resources for the implementation of plans.[3] The large population size facilitates the mobilization and concentration of manpower, so that construction can proceed speedily without damaging routine production operations. Before Land Reform, arable lands were owned by rich landlords but rented or leased to tenants. The absentee landlords did not involve themselves in production and thus had little interest in long-term

[1] "Revised Draft of the National Program of Agricultural Development, 1956-1967," in *A Collection of Documents on Socialist Education* (Peking: The People's Press, 1958), Vol. 1, p. 632 (in Chinese). See also *Jiangxi Daily*, September 8, 1957 (in Chinese).

[2] The population and area of the communes visited are as follow: Dali—69,000 persons and 72 sq. km, Doushan—57,934 persons and 115 sq. km, Luogang—28,000 persons and 95 sq. km, Huancheng—53,700 persons and 68 sq. km.

[3] Su Xing, *The Socialist Road for China's Agriculture* (Peking: The People's Press, 1976), pp. 91-93 (in Chinese).

planning in land and water conservancy. The tenants, who were generally very poor, seldom had the capital to improve the production conditions.[4] The private ownership of land, together with other factors such as blind faith in *feng-shui*,[5] family and kinsman ties, cliquism, etc., also hindered the development of water conservancy. The establishment of the collective ownership system minimized the obstacles to water conservancy, eliminating some entirely, and at the same time allowed the communes to unify planning operations while facilitating mobilization and concentration of local resources.

Secondly, the commune is a total political and social entity, under the Commune Party Committee's guidance and the Revolutionary Committee's management. Very often, the cadres have a multiplicity of responsibilities since party cadres may be at the same time administrative committee cadres, and production team and brigade cadres are members of the commune level committees, or one person has to head two or more functional divisions, etc. Hence state policies can be smoothly and flexibly carried out, as the structure facilitates the information flow, carrying out of instructions, ideological guidance and coordination. In addition, because commune level cadres have to participate in production work for at least sixty days per annum and lower level cadres are fully involved in production, their participation in frontline production deepens their understanding of the actual situation in the commune, brigade and production team, and also increases the interaction, and strengthens the linkage, between the cadres and the masses.

Water conservancy is both a local and a central responsibility, but projects carried out by different authority levels must be well coordinated, and the construction of large-scale projects by higher level units relies much on the support from lower level units. The three-level system of collective ownership, responsibility and administration (communes, brigades, production teams), and the subordination of lower level units to the higher level ones, are favorable to the working out of comprehensive water conservancy projects. Because plans of lower level collectives are subject to the approval by high level collectives, projects of various scale which are the responsibility of different units can be well coordinated. Coercive force exists within the three-level system and this facilitates the mobilization of resources for necessary constructions.

Therefore, under the commune institution, small local projects can be carried out independently by brigades or production teams. The communes,

[4]Huang Zai-sheng, "The Study on the Mobilization of Manpower in China's Rural Communes—A Case Study" (Master's thesis, The Chinese University of Hong Kong, 1976), pp. 86-87.

[5]*Feng-shui* is the Chinese science of geomancy or the influence of landscape on people and their fortunes.

pooling their resources, may take charge of cross-brigade projects and may assist in the construction of large-scale cross-commune or cross-county projects as well.

SOME ILLUSTRATIONS

As the basic unit in the development of water conservation, the People's Commune has many advantages. The following examples of achievement in water conservancy within the past two decades are drawn from projects of various sizes which we visited in our trip to the south of Guangdong Province, the Zhu Jiang (Pearl River) Delta and adjacent areas in 1976 and 1978.

(A) Huancheng Commune in Xinhui County located at the lower reaches of Tanjiang has long been affected by floods and waterlogging. To improve agriculture, the commune fortified the embankments, replaced the original earth embankment with stone structures in some areas (in total, the commune has 46 km of major embankment and 500 km of supplementary embankment), and reclaimed fields from marshland (in total 300 *mu*).[6] The commune also mobilized its members, divided its land into six sections (*dawei*), and from 1975 onwards harnessed one section during the off-season of each year. Work involved included the complete reorganization of the irrigation and drainage system, construction of water locks and pumping stations, strengthening embankments and dredging water courses, land reclamation and reformation, and setting up high and low voltage electricity distribution systems. In this way the construction in Gonglu Dawei and Dongjia Dawei was completed. The major construction work of the Gonglu Dawei was carried out in the off-season of 1975-76. At that time, the commune mobilized a working force of 23,330 people, and finished the work in 23½ days. After improvement in production conditions had been made, agricultural production in Gonglu Dawei increased by 10 per cent in 1976, and, on average, the paddy fields yielded 800 to 900 *jin* per *mu*, some even increasing to 1,100 *jin* per *mu*.[7]

With irrigation and drainage problems solved, farmers can practice more intensive farming. For example, winter wheat is raised in paddy fields after the autumn harvest; fruits and other cash crops are grown on embankments. Land reformation and the setting up of electricity distribution systems also facilitate the mechanization of farming operations. Farming in 60 per cent of the fields in the commune has been mechanized. The replacement of human labor by electricity in pumping also saves considerable manpower for other work.[8] In

[6] 1 *mu* = 1/15 hectare.

[7] 1 *jin* = ½ kilogram.

[8] To irrigate one *mu* of paddy field by human labor requires 8 man-day per cropping on average; but requires only 0.05 man-day by electric pump (Huang, *op. cit.*, p. 158).

addition, the improvement of inland navigation facilitates the transportation of agricultural products.

(B) Dali Commune in Nanhai County has constructed reservoirs, reorganized its irrigation and drainage system, set up electricity transformation plants, electrical pumping stations and mobile pumping units since the establishment of the commune in the late 1950s. The commune, in joint efforts with other communes in the area, also strengthened embankments and built water gates to relieve threats of flood from the tributaries of the Zhu Jiang. For example, the Beicun Gate (128 m long, 8 m wide, with 21 sliding doors) was jointly constructed by Dali, Lishui, and Yanbu Communes to prevent floods from the Zhu Jiang. The construction was completed within a period of six months in 1959 with the participation of over 10,000 people. When finished, more than 100,000 *mu* of fields in the area benefited from it. The Beicun Gate, together with the Shakou Gate near Foshan City, keep Zhu Jiang and Xi Jiang flood waters under control in the Dali Commune.

In 1974, the commune again organized over 10,000 members to implement the Chang Hongling Project. The Project which included the construction of a pumping station and an aqueduct (9 m long), brought water from the Xianxi Reservoir to a service reservoir 38 m higher on a hill; from there, water flowed around eleven hills along the aqueduct. Thus the irrigation problem in the eastern hilly area of the commune was solved, slopes were transformed into terraces (in total 1,300 *mu*) for the planting of oranges and mandarins, and this increased the acreage of cultivated lands immensely.

By and large, the commune has overcome most of its irrigation and drainage problems. To further increase the acreage of fields and to prevent the loss of irrigation water caused by evaporation, the commune is now planning to develop an underground irrigation system. The development of water conservancy, land reformation and the mechanization of farming operations (now in 80 per cent of the commune's land) have improved production conditions. The per unit area output of foodstuff has been tripled as compared to the pre-liberation period (1,400 *jin* per *mu* at present). In addition, more and more manpower has been released from farming, and diverted to production operations in other sectors.

(C) Doushan Commune in Taishan county in the past suffered greatly from drought and tidal floods from Nanhai (South Sea). Between 1955 and 1962, eight reservoirs were constructed within the commune's area (6 at commune level and 2 at brigade level, with a total capacity of approximately 7,500,000 m^3). At the same time, the commune participated in the construction of four county level reservoirs (1 in 1960, 2 in 1961 and 1 in 1973, with a total capacity of approximately 32,000,000 m^3). At present, 54,000 *mu* of cultivated lands in the commune benefit from these reservoirs as the supply of 1,000 m^3/mu yearly can guarantee sufficient irrigation water for growing crops even in years of long drought.

Dalongdong Reservoir is the largest reservoir in the area (catchment area: 148 km^2, capacity: 250,000,000 m^3, increased to 35,000,000 m^3 in 1977). The Reservoir was constructed in 1958, jointly by Doushan, Guanghai, Chonglou and Duanfen Communes. Over 10,000 people were mobilized by the four communes in the off-season; apart from that, 1,000 to 1,500 people stayed on site during the whole construction period of thirteen months. This reservoir is multi-functional. Besides its flood detention and irrigation func-tions, hydro-electric power (a station of 2,500 kilowatts capacity), fresh-water fishery (30,000 jin of yield yearly), and forestry (100,000 mu of plantation) have also been developed in the area.

As a matter of fact, Dalondong Reservoir is a major component of the Fenghuojiao Water Conservancy Scheme which is a county level project. The Scheme, with twelve reservoirs of various sizes, services a total area of 270,000 mu of cultivated land in the six communes of the region.

Another major component of the Scheme is the Fenghuojiao Gate at the estuary of Sanhehai, 17 km from Doushan Town. The Gate, with forty-eight sliding doors (each 3.2 m wide), operating by motors and with locks for ships up to 2,000 tons, was constructed in 1959, through the joint efforts of members of the Doushan, Guanghai, Chonglou, Duanfen, Doufu, Chixi Com-munes, as well as factory workers, soldiers, and administrative cadres in the region. After two years of work, the Gate was built, protecting 275,000 mu of cultivated land in the six communes from tidal floods in the typhoon season.

The implementation of the Fenghuojiao Scheme, together with the con-struction of reservoirs within the commune's area, has basically solved the difficulties in irrigation and flood control faced by Doushan Commune in the past. To further improve the production conditions, Doushan Commune has also undertaken a series of operations. These include reorganization and dredging of its irrigation and drainage system, strengthening the embankment, division of cultivated lands into small portions (wei) of 100 mu each (one portion for each production team) surrounding each portion with embank-ments, installation of more electrical pumping stations and mobile pumping units, land leveling and reformation, etc. Due to efforts the commune has made, the acreage of cultivated land has increased from 36,000 mu in the pre-liberation period to 68,000 mu at present, of which 62,000 mu are paddy fields. All single-cropping fields have been changed to double-cropping, and on the average, the multiple crop index is currently 233 per cent. In 1977, the production of foodstuff per mu was 1,051 jin on the average, three times that in 1958. In the old days, Doushan area could never produce sufficient foodstuff for local consumption, but now there is a surplus for export.

(D) The Dashahe Reservoir, lying between Kaiping, Xinxing, and Enping Counties is a cross-county project. Under the supervision and coordination of the Kaiping County authority, the joint effort of eight communes in the area brought the Reservoir to completion. The construction, started in August 1958, was completed in 1959. The eight communes mobilized, at the peak-time of construction, over 12,000 people to participate; and on the average, 6,000 people were working daily when the dams were under construction.

With a catchment area of 237 km² and a water surface of 28 km², the major functions of the Reservoir are irrigation and generation of hydro-electric power. A total of 145,700 *mu* of cultivated land in eight communes (77 brigades, or 860 production teams) is irrigated by the Reservoir; another 60,000 *mu* has been relieved from threat of flooding. The four hydro-electric power stations of the Reservoir have in total a capacity of 2,140 kilowatts, supplying electricity mainly to their own region. In addition, forestry (over 2,000 *mu* of plantation), fresh-water fishery (200 *mu* of water surface, 300,000 *jin* of yield yearly), farming and livestock raising are carried out within the administrative boundaries of the Reservoir.

Since the completion of the Dashahe Reservoir, a significant improvement in agriculture has been observed in Kaiping County. In the past, fields were flooded whenever 200 mm of precipitation was recorded in a day. The production of foodstuffs satisfied local consumption only for three months. But now floods are controlled, and there is surplus in the production of foodstuff.

(E) The Heshan Hydro-electric Power Station in Kaiping County is one of the nine major components of the Jin Jiang Water Conservancy Scheme. The completion of this station which is under the management of the Foshan District Water Conservancy Bureau also relied on the joint effort and support of communes in Kaiping and Enping Counties. In late 1970, the authority organized more than 23,000 people of the two counties to start the scheme. In September of 1974, basic construction work was completed. This included opening a new waterway (880 m long and 6 m wide) and construction of a concrete dam (with 4 gate doors, each 5.3 m wide) on the new waterway, an inflatable nylon dam on the old course, a shiplock, and a hydro-electric power station of 1,250 kilowatts capacity.

This multi-functional station protects the region from floods, and its electricity supply also facilitates the electrification of the irrigation and drainage system. Most paddy fields in the area have been changed from single-cropping to double-cropping, and their production has increased rapidly, from 100-200 *jin* to 1,000 *jin* a year per *mu*. Steamboats up to 50 tons can sail easily through the Heshan Gorge, and the motor road on the watergate brigade links the two sides of the river. Thus, communication and the transportation of agricultural and industrial products as well as raw materials have been greatly facilitated.

In general, water conservancy projects are multi-functional as they may involve irrigation, flood control, drainage, hydro-electricity generation, transportation, etc., in combination with land reformation, reclamation of new arable lands, and the setting up of electricity distribution systems. Such development not only creates favorable conditions for the mechanization and modernization of agriculture, but also puts water resources to full use in industry and commerce.

Among the above examples, some are commune level projects, while others are under the management of the county authority or even the district authority. While commune level projects must rely on the efforts of the commune concerned, the construction of cross-commune or higher level projects also depends on the support of individual communes.

The next question, then, is how and why the People's Commune is able to develop its potential, mobilize its manpower and resources for construction.

ORGANIZATION AND MOBILIZATION FOR CONSTRUCTION

While the People's Commune institution has created favorable conditions for water conservancy development, the communes still have to face the difficulty of limited resources. As illustrated by the examples in the previous section, the communes are well able to cope with problems and are self-reliant. Obviously, they do not rely on investment from outside, but instead depend on their own labor force and whatever other limited resources they have.[9] However, whether the potential of the communes can be fully developed depends upon "how works are planned and how well the masses are organized."

These are the major characteristics of work organization in water conservancy construction as they appear at present:

1. Localization

Water conservancy projects are mainly local. Every administrative unit is responsible for constructions within its boundary. The communes provide a good illustration of this. They are the basic planning units which much allow for needs and conditions which may differ greatly from region to region. The

[9]Command Office of Basic Construction of Farmland in Guangdong Province, *Speeches on the Basic Construction of Farmland* (Guangdong: The People's Press, 1976), pp. 17-29 (in Chinese).

communes must coordinate individual construction carried out by brigades and production teams within their administrative boundaries; at the same time they have to contribute to projects undertaken by higher administrative level units when they stand to benefit from the scheme.

For their water conservancy projects, the local people usually participate actively in the whole process. Their participation usually begins at the very lowest level and continues through all stages of development—from planning to implementation to maintenance. They are not simply workers for a certain project; they are members of responsible collectives who hold real power.

Aside from the leading cadres and the masses, construction also involves the use of local technicians who in their work rely heavily on native methods. Since there are in any commune technicians with considerable experience, these can be used to train others. Thus the experienced technicians train and supervise apprentice technicians. The employment of native methods is a realistic policy for this reason: Western methods necessitate a substantial investment in machinery and equipment.

Localization of water conservancy motivates the people to work for the collective, facilitates the mobilization of the masses and the concentration of resources, thus enabling the communes to assume responsibility for projects. In addition, dividing responsibility according to administrative boundaries or geographical criteria and allowing regional organizations to coordinate functional programs in an area can minimize the conflicts between functional organizations.[10]

2. Ideological guidance

The peasant culture, behavioral conservatism, fatalism, familism and superstition all hinder the development of water conservancy.[11] The cadres' efforts in ideological guidance—through criticism, work and leadership[12]—not only remove such ideological impediments, but direct the members to put the common good first instead of aiming at individual material rewards. Furthermore, the high demonstrability of collective strength in water conservancy may also bring about a better ideological attitude among the masses.

[10] L. D. James and R. R. Lee, *Economics of Water Resources Planning* (New York: McGraw-Hall, 1971), pp. 137-140.

[11] United Nations, *Proceedings of the Symposium on Social and Non-Economic Factors in Water Resources Development* (New York: United Nations, 1976), Water Resources Series No. 47, pp. 22-24.

[12] *Speeches on the Basic Construction of Farmland*, p. 21; Zhong Zhiqing, *With Class Struggle as the Key, Popularize Tachai County as Soon as Possible* (Guangdong: The People's Press, 1976), pp. 44-52 (in Chinese).

3. Integration of water conservancy organizations with administrative organizations

Organizations involved in water conservancy construction may be divided into two types, namely "established" and "task-oriented" organizations. The former include water conservancy offices at different administrative levels. For example, at the commune level there is the water conservancy society which is made up of technical personnel. And in some communes such as Doushan, there exists also a "battalion for basic construction of farmlands" which is a militia form of organization specializing in water conservancy and related projects, and a consultation committee on water conservancy and farmlands. The "task-oriented" organizations include the "command" set up on construction sites, "specialized teams" and the masses organized in the forms of "battalions" and "companies" which are formed only for a specific period of time and for a specific construction task. The water conservancy society is a unit under the commune administration, while the "specialized teams," "battalions" and "companies" are administrative-unit based organizations led by administrative cadres. Although the various organizations may differ in form, responsibility and capability, through the three-in-one method (under the leadership of cadres, assisted by local technical personnel, with the participation of the masses) in both the planning and implementation stages, they are well integrated, coordinated and supervised by the commune administration. The cadres who form the planning and implementation stages are well integrated, coordinated and supervised by the commune administration. The cadres who form the nucleus of leadership, the technical personnel from water conservancy offices who assist in planning and on construction sites, together with the masses who are well organized are integrated into one powerful unity for the purpose of implementing plans.

4. Militarized organization

When the masses have to be mobilized to participate in construction work, the brigades are usually taken as basic units of organization. Under the leadership of a "command" set up on site, participants are organized into battalions and companies. Militia and party cadres from "break-through teams" are expected to handle difficult and dangerous tasks. Different types of operations are labeled as "general mobilization," "combat disposition," "exterminating combat" and "surprise attack," etc. The employment of military terms and forms of organization strengthens the organization of participants, ensures discipline, efficient mobilization and the close coordination of all.

5. Unification, centralization and flexibility in operation

The communes, through coordination of industrial, agricultural, trade, educational and military affairs, through unification in ideology, command, timing, action and planning, and through centralization in leadership, manpower, capital, materials and tools, are in a good position to solve the problems related to resources and manpower. Under the coordination of the commune, various sectors can get together to help each other while providing their individual contribution of manpower. For example, manufacturing industries provide more raw material and tools, commercial units ensure commodities and material supplies, high school pupils with basic training in surveying participate on construction sites, and so on.

Since the shortage of machinery must be remedied through the use of manpower, two forms of task-oriented organizations have been adopted: (a) Forming brigade-based specialized teams which would not draw too much manpower away from production (usually 10-15 per cent) to work all year round;[13] (b) For construction which needs abundant labor, the brigade is the basic unit which provides the manpower. Depending on need, a number of brigades are centrally mobilized during the off-season. Through unified action and timing, the construction work can thus be completed within a short period of time.

The aim of manpower policy in the water conservancy context is to utilize manpower rationally and fully, to minimize the dislocation of routine production, and to tackle conservancy projects one by one.

6. Reciprocity based on equality and mutual benefit

Though financial assistance may come from the county in some cases (e.g., the total expenditure for the Gonglu Dawei project in Huancheng Commune was 530,000 *yuan* of which 8,000 *yuan* was contributed by Xinhui County), usually the commune itself is responsible for capital, material and manpower needed for construction within its boundaries. The same holds for brigades and production teams. However, some units, particularly at the brigade or lower levels, may lack sufficient manpower and resources to complete their projects within a short period of time without disrupting normal production. In such cases, other units may come to their aid provided that some reciprocity is extended in the future.

The Gonglu Dawei Project is a good example of this. If the eight brigades of Gonglu Dawei had relied only on their own manpower it would have taken them at least four years to complete the job, with a yield loss of 720,000 *jin* per harvest. But with the participation of other brigades in the commune, the construction was completed in one off-season without affecting other production activities. Of course, the brigades in Gonglu Dawei have to contribute, in

---

[13] *Speeches on the Basic Construction of Farmland*, p. 15.

their turn, to construction carried out later in other sections (*dawei*).

Work done by each brigade is recorded. When the construction in all the six sections (*dawei*) is completed in the future, the commune administration will compare the relative contribution and gains of each brigade. Any imbalance will then be rectified.

For other collective projects, whether they are commune-level projects (e.g., the Chang Hongling Project in Dali Commune), cross-commune, or cross-county projects (e.g., the Fenghuojiao Water Conservancy Scheme and the Dashahe Reservoir), the units involved all contribute in proportion to the benefits expected. It is through the cooperation of different collectivities that the water conservancy projects of various scales can be carried out efficiently.

From the above observations, it may be said that water conservancy construction in China does not depend on heavy investment from the state; in other words, it is not capital-intensive. Instead, it relies greatly on the mobilization of local manpower and resources. But, while the large rural population is certainly important in bringing water conservancy construction to completion, this task cannot be regarded as entirely labor-intensive either. With plans and definite principles, the leaders systematically mobilize and organize the masses, concentrate the resources, make proper use of them, and spur construction teams into action. It is through this organization-intensive method[14] that the people's commune can develop its potential, solve problems in manpower and resources, and obtain positive results in water conservancy.

DISCUSSION

Progress and economic development of a society depend much on rational planning and the efforts of the people. However, social development and economic growth cannot be treated separately, but must be integrated at all levels for sustained development. Improvement in the national economy and the livelihood of individuals relate to how social structural problems are handled. Planned social change involves eliminating inequality in terms of wealth or opportunity, removing all the constraints of traditional society, and mobilizing the masses to participate actively. Unless these problems are solved, all-round development can never be attained.

The example of water conservancy construction in China demonstrates the necessity of integrated social and economic planning for development objectives. Water conservancy is a means to enhance the development of rural economy from its base. The establishment of the communes as political and social units greatly changes the structure of human relationships in rural communities and makes it possible to organize water conservancy projects. The

[14] A concept suggested by Dr. C. K. Yang of the University of Pittsburgh.

methods adopted by the communes are neither capital-intensive nor labor-intensive, but organization-intensive. Organization-intensity implies labor-intensity and maximized utilization of available resources; the organization framework has a guiding function. The highly integrated working force can ensure efficiency and allow a large degree of operational flexibility, thus enabling the communes to coordinate and carry out water conservancy projects within their boundaries and assist in building up large-scale state-run projects.

It is questionable whether the organization-intensive method can completely solve such problems as shortages in resources, difficulties in work coordination, and lowering of production during the construction period. It is also difficult to assess the durability of constructions by native methods and to determine whether they should be replaced by modern installations in the future.

At the present stage, however, we can see that the communes have made all-round water conservancy possible. The advantages of these projects can be counted not only in primary but also in secondary benefits. Water conservancy transforms manpower capital into fixed capital.[15] It promotes the full use of arable lands and facilitates mechanization, electrification and application of chemurgy; it also helps to develop sideline production, economize manpower utilization in the agriculture sector, as well as provide energy and transportation facilities. The rise of productivity in agriculture increases individual income and collective capital accumulation. It also provides more raw material, manpower, and a market for industry. The increase in acreage of cultivated land, the development of industry and other sideline production can absorb the relative labor surplus, including seasonal surplus and underutilized labor. Thus the basic contradiction of modernization, mechanization, and manpower utilization is solved.

So far, it is still difficult to assess quantitatively how much water conservancy has contributed to the production rise in various sectors. However, it is undeniable that since favorable conditions are created, agriculture and rural enterprises stand to benefit. Furthermore, rural economic growth leads to a rise in collective income. Thus, the collectivities can give more assistance to less developed lower level units. Consequently, the difference among collectivities (between rural communities, rural and urban, industrial and agricultural) may be reduced.

The success in water conservancy illustrates the dynamic nature of communes, and shows how communes are capable of linking social and economic progress. How far the Chinese organization-intensive model can be applied to other developing countries with scarce resources but ample manpower remains to be seen.

[15] Huang, *op. cit.*, p. 22.

CHAPTER SIX

China's Economic Development Experience: Consolidation and Experimentation in the Post-cultural Revolution Phase

Joseph Yu-shek Cheng

Economic development has been a very important part of socialist construction which formed the major task of the Chinese people after the establishment of the People's Republic of China in 1949. But socialist construction is considerably more than nation-building plus economic development, it also incorporates the ideal of moving towards communism, and socialist construction is intended to bring about the materialistic and non-materialistic conditions necessary for the realization of communism.

In the wake of the Cultural Revolution, when intense political activities gave way to normalization, the Chinese leadership finally managed to devote a considerable part of its attention to economic issues. During the Cultural Revolution, certain anarchist tendencies emerged: the party and the administrative structures were totally discredited, industrial discipline broke down and economic production was ignored. Yet the Chinese leadership's tasks in the post-Cultural Revolution phase were not simply limited to the restoration of work discipline, the establishment of a new pattern of management and the promotion of economic production. The Maoist ideals of self-reduction of the "three major gaps" between the living standards—of urban and rural areas, of workers and peasants, and of those doing manual work and those doing mental work—which had been made the political orthodoxy in the Cultural Revolution had to be incorporated in the Chinese economic planning process and development policies. This is why the Chinese economic development experience in the post-Cultural Revolution years may best be characterized as that of a period of consolidation and experimentation. This chapter, however, does not intend to analyze the developments in China since the fall of the Gang of Four and limits itself to the period of 1968-76.

The search for an economic development strategy appropriate for China probably began at the end of China's First Five-Year Plan (1953-57) when the Chinese leadership became disillusioned with the blind imitation of the Soviet model. In a major piece of Chairman Mao's work, "On the Ten Major

Relationships," which was an important speech made at the Politburo in 1956, at least five of the ten relationships discussed were concerned with the Chinese economy and the search for a development strategy appropriate for China.[1] They were:

1. the relationship between industry and agriculture and between heavy and light industry;
2. the relationship between industry in the coastal regions and industry in the interior;
3. the relationship between economic construction and defence construction;
4. the relationship between the state, the units of production and the individual producers;
5. the relationship between the center and the regions.

Though put forward as a response to the unsatisfactory consequences of following the Soviet model—attempting to achieve rapid industrialization with emphasis on the development of heavy industries at the expense of light industries and agriculture—the above five major relationships (or "contradictions" in Chinese communist terminology) remained central to all economic debates during the following twenty years. Policy controversies regarding the handling of these contradictions were largely responsible for the emergence of the "two roads," the struggle between the "two roads" and the radical zigzags in development policies. It was also the handling of these five contradictions which would determine the pattern of socialist transition in China and to what extent the Chinese development experience would constitute an alternative model for the Third World.

There was probably little disagreement among the Chinese leaders that all positive elements and all available forces had to be mobilized to build a socialist society in a "faster, better and more economical way." Struggles concerning Liu Shao-ch'i's "revisionist" economic policies in the 1960s, the importation of foreign technology in the 1970s, Teng Hsiao-p'ing's alleged re-imposition of direct and exclusive ministerial control over enterprises shortly before Mao's death and the activities of the Gang of Four did not hinge on considerations of the absolute growth rate of China's GNP but on the process of socialist transition, with the attendant danger of capitalist retrogression. An examination of the above five contradictions form the basis of this chapter.

[1] Stuart Schram (ed.), *Mao Tse-tung Unrehearsed* (Harmondsworth: Penguin Books, 1974), pp. 61-83. This speech of Mao was first made public officially in December 1976 and has been given much attention since. An English translation of the official version may be found in *Peking Review*, Vol. 20, No. 1 (January 1, 1977), pp. 10-25.

GENERAL STRATEGY

In 1969, when the normalization process after the Culture Revolution gradually began to gain acceptance, two important statements on Chinese development policies were released.[2] Both statements reaffirmed the policy of "agriculture as the foundation, and industry as the leading factor," along with the principles of "self-reliance," "walking on two legs" and fostering technological innovations.

In this context, three trends deserve considerable attention. First, in view of the Soviet invasion of Czechoslovakia, the enunciation of the Brezhnev doctrine and the Sino-Soviet border clashes, there was a predictable emphasis on integrating industrial construction with preparation for war. Secondly, the strategy of taking "agriculture as the foundation, and industry as the leading factor" received much greater clarification and elaboration. All units were called upon to support agriculture, and an industrial network was to be established to serve it. Mechanization of agriculture was regarded as vital, and workshops for the manufacture and repair of agricultural machinery were to be established in every county. Thirdly, it was indicated that, when formulating production plans, "it is necessary to mobilise the masses and see to it that there is enough leeway." The introduction of the concept of "leeway" at this stage suggested that a compromise might have been reached between planners who were calling for limited goals and cautious planning and those who claimed that the Cultural Revolution had released incalculable productive energies which should be allowed free rein.

The theme of integrating industrial construction with preparation for war meant that every area, province and city, should pay attention to rational geographical distribution and appropriate multi-purpose development of industries in line with Chairman Mao's instruction: "Various localities should endeavor to build up independent industrial systems."

A rational geographical distribution of industries would certainly be concerned with the proper handling of the relationship between industry in the coastal regions and industry in the interior. Chinese industries were and still are far too concentrated in the North East and along the coast. By the early 1970s, a few major cities—Shenyang, Tientsin, Anshan, Lu-shun/Talien, Tsingtao, Peking, Shanghai and Kwangchow produced almost half of the country's total value of industrial output; and Shanghai alone produced about

---

[2] See *People's Daily* editorial, February 21, 1969; English translation in *Peking Review*, Vol. 12, No. 9 (February 28, 1969), pp. 4-6; and an article by the Writing Group of the Peking Municipal Revolutionary Committee, *Red Flag*, No. 19 (1969); English translation in *Peking Review*, Vol. 12, No. 43 (October 24, 1969), pp. 7-13.

15.5 per cent of the total.[3] On the other hand, the vast interior—the North West, the South West and Inner Mongolia—had very few industries. This imbalance surely had to be redressed. But it involved much more than that. In preparing for war against the Soviet Union, logic would suggest that heavy industrial plants in the North East and North West should be moved to Central and South China. The heavy concentration of industries in a few urban centers along the coast, both from the military viewpoint and that of a rational geographical distribution, required appropriate adjustment. Thus, in late 1969 and early 1970, there was considerable speculation regarding the re-distribution of China's industries.

It was said that the Chinese government planned to move industrial plants from "the first line" (east of Chengchow and including Shenyang, Tsingtao, Shanghai, Foochow, Kwangchow, etc.) to "the second line" (west of Chengchow including Sian, Chungking, Kweiyang, Kunming, etc.). It was also reported that new industrial centers were to be established in the five provinces of Hunan, Hupei, Honan, Hopei and Anhwei and that industrial plants were to be gradually transported to these new centers from the coastal areas and the North East. These reports were never substantially confirmed, though they were backed up by sporadic evidence.

To implement such a rational geographical distribution of industries, certain measures of inter-regional resource distribution had to be imposed by the center. Highly industrialized areas such as Shanghai and Liaoning remitted to the center well over half of their annual revenue while less developed regions typically not only retained all of their revenue but also frequently received additional direct subsidies from the central government. In the least developed provinces and autonomous regions, these subsidies financed over half of all provincial and local expenditure. The central government not only redistributed substantial fiscal resources, but also systematically transferred skilled labor and technical and managerial manpower from more developed regions (particularly Shanghai) to less developed areas. By the early 1970s, Shanghai had supplied over half a million skilled workers to inland industry.[4] Though these measures had been carried out since 1949, it seemed that the pace was speeded up after the Cultural Revolution.

Besides preparing for war and striving for a better inter-regional balance, a

---

[3] For an analysis of the "weight" of each province in the gross value of China's industrial output, see Robert M. Field, Nicholas R. Nicholas and John P. Emerson, "A Reconstruction of the Gross Value of Industrial Output by Province in the People's Republic of China: 1949-1973," *Foreign Economic Reports* (U.S. Department of Commerce), No. 7 (July 1975), p. 16.

[4] Alexander Eckstein, *China's Economic Development* (Ann Arbor: University of Michigan Press, 1975), p. 364.

rational geographical distribution of industries also aimed at correcting a number of anomalies. In the first place, many Chinese industrial centers were too far away from the sources of raw materials and fuels as well as from the consumers. For example, Shanghai, the largest textile center with a production capacity of 40 per cent of the Chinese total, had to import about 60 to 70 per cent of the cotton it needed from Hunan, Hopei and Shantung. In addition, Shanghai had to import millions of tons of coal from North China.[5] It was only logical, therefore, to develop textile centers in the cotton growing areas in North China to minimize costs and to reduce their reliance on textile products from Shanghai; at the same time, it also paid to develop small collieries near Shanghai to increase its self-sufficiency in fuel. In view of the bottlenecks in transportation, these investment plans appeared all the more urgent. Moreover, even within the same region, imbalances still existed among the various sectors of the same industry. The mining of iron ore was well developed, for example, in the North East, largely due to the legacy of the Japanese occupation. Consequently that region's mining capacity exceeded that of steel-making, and the latter exceeded that of rolling. Steel, therefore, had to be imported from Japan while iron ore and cast iron were exported to the same country. Simultaneously, the rolling mills and machine-building plants in East China had to bring in cast iron and finished steel from outside the region. To remedy the situation, industrial plants, wherever possible, were to be established near the sources of raw materials and fuel and the population centers where the industrial products were consumed. This would help to ensure the full utilization of natural resources, the elimination of unnecessary transport costs and the acceleration of economic turnover. Secondly, in order to reduce the differences in living standards between peasants and industrial workers and between urban and rural areas, new industrial centers were to be built in rural areas. These industrial centers would also help to improve agriculture by supplying much-needed inputs such as tractors, farm machinery, chemical fertilizers, pesticides, etc. Thirdly, to speed up the economic development in national minority areas (largely in the North West and South West), priority was to be given to industrial development in those areas. This was essential not only to raise the low living standards in minority areas, but to help implement Mao Tse-tung's policy of eliminating "Han chauvinism" and the centrifugal tendencies among certain national minorities, particularly those living near the Sino-Soviet border. Finally, while striving to achieve self-sufficiency, each region and locality was at the same time to specialize in products most appropriate to its factor endowments.

The establishment of independent industrial systems in local areas also

[5] Hsu Tak-ming, *Communist Chinese Economy After the Cultural Revolution* (Hong Kong: Union Research Institute, 1974), p. 259.

meant a solid implementation of Mao's policy of "walking on two legs" and an emphasis on local small-scale factories. Back in the Great Leap Forward, the development of local industries had received special attention and plans were made to establish factories in every county and every commune. Due to mismanagement and financial losses, however, most of these factories were closed down after the Great Leap. In fact, the "70 Guidelines for Industry," authorized by Liu Shao-ch'i, ordered all local factories and mines incurring losses to be abandoned. In the early 1970s, some of these local enterprises still survived and expanded through ploughing back profits and improvising out of their own resources rather than relying on state investment grants.

This growth of enterprise self-sufficiency was particularly marked with regard to machinery. Numerous factories in all branches of industry reportedly made or even invented their own equipment rather than getting outside help. This process has been criticized by Audrey Donnithorne as "unnecessarily extravagant" since time and effort were spent discovering what was already known in larger and more modern enterprises.[6] Nevertheless, since local plants had to rely on local resources, the known technology and equipment usually had to be imported into the locality. They might themselves be in short supply in the advanced industrial sector. Such inputs, moreover, might not be suitable for local needs. The principle of self-reliance required local industries to be based on technology which made optimal use of natural resources, manpower and equipment which were available locally. Furthermore, the immense educational value of developing local technology was not to be underestimated, particularly since educated youth from the urban areas would almost inevitably be involved.

As indicated by Jon Sigurdson, two measures were important in fostering technology appropriate for local industries and rural economic development:

1. The development of "entirely" new technologies in research and design institutes as exemplified by the design of chemical fertilizer plants;
2. The use of old designs and processes and second-hand machinery appropriate to the scale of operations and needs of the localities.[7]

The significance for rural industries of this development and transfer of technology can best be appreciated by an examination of the linkages between agriculture, rural and modern industry. Rural industry was introduced as a

[6] Audrey Donnithorne, "China's Cellular Economy: Some Economic Trends Since the Cultural Revolution," *The China Quarterly*, No. 52 (September–December 1972), p. 610.

[7] Jon Sigurdson, "Rural Industry and the Internal Transfer of Technology," in Stuart Schram (ed.), *Authority, Participation and Cultural Change in China* (London: Cambridge University Press, 1973), pp. 223-224.

transmission belt for scientific and technological knowledge. Initially, the linkage with modern industry was mainly a one-way relationship, in which rural industry was provided with much of the necessary technology and equipment. The linkage between agriculture and rural industry, on the other hand, was a mutual relationship. Rural industry, for its part, provided an increasing amount of inputs into agriculture and was responsible for the formation of technical skills in that sector. Agriculture in turn supplied raw materials and capital. As the level of agricultural production rose and rural industries expanded in scale and improved in sophistication, the differences between the rural and modern industrial sectors would gradually be reduced. Under normal circumstances, a local industrial system would be best able to serve the local rural sector. Indeed, the division of labor within local industrial systems revealed that local industries were chiefly designed to serve agriculture.

THE RURAL SECTOR

In the agricultural sector, the campaign to expand and merge communes and production brigades, which started in October 1968, and the talk of a "flying leap" in agricultural production, which reached its peak in late 1969, gradually gave way to a more cautious approach as China entered the 1970s. The emphasis then was entirely on gradual development with no sudden changes in the existing pattern of commune organization. In the Constitution promulgated in 1975, it was clearly stated that the production team would be the basic accounting unit.[8]

In rural areas, major efforts were concentrated on water conservation works, mechanization, electrification, and small chemical plants. Such developments were made possible by the official requirement for industry to support agriculture. Although the principle of self-reliance was given much emphasis, and almost all investment funds had to come from the communes themselves, it is also obvious that very considerable resources in the industrial sector were devoted to supplying agriculture with the modern inputs that it required. As revealed in Premier Chou En-lai's "Report on the Work of the Government" delivered at the Fourth National People's Congress in early 1975: while China's gross industrial output for 1974 was estimated to be 190 per cent more than 1964, electric power was said to be 200 per cent more, chemical fertilizers 330 per cent more, and tractors 520 per cent more.[9] A significant

---

[8] See the Constitution of the People's Republic of China adopted in January 1975; English translation in *Peking Review*, Vol. 18, No. 4 (January 24, 1975), p. 14.

[9] See Chou En-lai, "Report on the Work of the Government," delivered at the Fourth National People's Congress in January 1975; English translation in *Peking Review*, Vol. 18, No. 4 (January 24, 1975), p. 22.

proportion of the electric power, chemical fertilizers and tractors did not come from the advanced industrial sector, but was produced by small plants in the county. Nonetheless these plants still required machinery, equipment, spare parts and other inputs from the advanced industrial sector. More important still, precious foreign exchange was spent in the U. S. and Japan in the early 1970s for the purchase of modern chemical fertilizer plants.

A major campaign to build water works started in the winter of 1968-69, and in eleven provinces (including Liaoning, Hopei, Hunan and Kwangsi), 37 million people were mobilized. The operative slogan was "conservation, small-ness of scale and self-reliance"; and this resulted in the construction of numerous small reservoirs. Central large-scale projects, however, were financed by the state, as in the case of the Kiangtu irrigation project in Kiangsu.

As Chairman Mao pointed out: "The fundamental way out for agriculture lies in mechanization." Certainly progress in this field was not to be neglected; and major efforts were made to establish a farm machinery repair shop in every county. Thus, after a few years of relative quiescence in the design and manufacture of new farm machinery, an exhibition was held in Nanning, Kwangsi, in May 1969 to introduce a new rice transplanter. There were many similar exhibitions in the years which followed, which indicated a continuing concern with rural mechanization.

The rural electrification scheme was based mainly on the development of hydro-electric power. Most of the small hydro-electric power stations in the countryside were financed by the communes and the production brigades, and usually had a generating capacity of between 20 and 100 kilowatts. In the use of electricity, priority had to be given first to irrigation networks, then rural industries, and, last of all, domestic consumption.

The chemical fertilizer industry was perhaps the most successful of all the small-scale rural industries. According to an estimate by Chao Kang, in 1974, 45 per cent of the total chemical fertilizer output in China came from these small rural plants.[10] This increase in production in the rural areas, plus the importation of modern plants, could significantly reduce China's purchases from abroad, notably from Japan. Indeed, China might perhaps achieve self-sufficiency in the near future.

Since all these developments were largely to be financed locally, the problem of accumulating local funds became very serious. Here there were dangers as well as bright prospects. It appeared, in most cases, that grain production alone could not raise sufficient funds to provide for these developments; there was a need to generate further income from sideline production. The importance of sideline production and the need to pay appropriate attention

[10]Chao Kang, "The Production and Application of Chemical Fertilizers in China," *The China Quarterly*, No. 64 (December 1975), p. 713.

to such sectors as forestry and animal husbandry (particularly pig raising, both collective and private) became apparent. Yet over-emphasis on these activities, it was feared, would "give rise to capitalism"; consequently some local cadres became "hesitant, gave no strong leadership, and lacked enthusiasm." There was also a genuine and legitimate concern regarding "spontaneous" rural capitalism and possessiveness among peasants.

The almost total reliance on the local accumulation of funds meant that the richer communes would be able to do much better than the poorer communes and this might help to perpetuate and even sharpen the disparities in wealth between communes, counties and larger regions. This danger, of course, could be remedied by the state contributing to the financing of such projects in the poor regions; but there is no evidence to show that this was being done, except perhaps in the national minority areas.

Both the need to finance local projects and to employ rationally the income derived from rural industries might help to increase the status of brigade and commune as economic units. Nevertheless, as indicated above, there appeared no signs that the Chinese wanted to speed up the process. In fact, Chairman Mao stated in the early 1960s that movement from production team ownership to commune ownership should not occur until the latter's own income was greater than one half of the gross income of all three levels.[11]

THE INDUSTRIAL SECTOR

After the political upheavals of the Cultural Revolution had abated, the Chinese leadership, confronted with problems of restoring labor discipline and incentives, was hard pressed to increase industrial output to make up for the losses of previous years. To promote production, a campaign of socialist emulation was launched by the Peking Iron and Steel Corporation in September 1969. In this campaign, though stress was placed on "revolutionary spirit," it was quite clear that the aim was to minimize waste, to economise on raw materials and fuel, and to utilize to the full existing productive capacity.[12]

The problem of waste was tackled boldly. In November 1969, Shanghai's industrial sector was said to have saved 900,000 tons of coal and vast amounts of electricity, steel, timber and petroleum in the previous ten months.[13] Efforts were made to recycle waste. This was facilitated by large-scale programs of inter-factory coordination, with the waste of one factory being used

[11] See "Reading Notes on the Soviet Union's Political Economies," as translated in *Miscellany of Mao Tse-tung's Thought (1949-1968)*, Joint Publications Research Service (JPRS), No. 61269-72, (February 20, 1974), p. 267.

[12] *People's Daily*, September 11, 1969, p. 1 and September 14, 1969, pp. 1 and 3.

[13] *Ibid.*, November 24, 1969.

by another. Such coordination was developed further in 1970 when production units, research units and schools combined to accomplish specific industrial projects, e.g., to manufacture a new product or develop a new technology. This was to be the precursor of independent regional industrial systems.

Technical innovation and improvements in product quality also received due attention. Though many technicians, removed during the Cultural Revolution, returned to their posts, this did not necessarily mean that there was a return to the former policy of reliance on "experts." Workers were to be involved in industrial design and technical innovation and former specialists were required to undergo reeducation through participation in collective labor. Groups and committees responsible for such innovations were set up, based on a "triple combination" of veteran workers, cadres and specialists and such innovations were examined by review committees in which workers participated. Workers were enjoined to supervise the implementation of new designs and to avoid the previous blind reliance on foreign blueprints. Care also was to be taken to ensure that new products went into production within one year of their being formally adopted.

The improvement of product quality was, therefore, of prime importance. It would remain a problem so long as factionalism and anarchism remained and so long as cadres had not regained sufficient confidence to take bold initiatives. It was also, perhaps, a consequence of emulation campaigns which stressed quantity rather than quality. To deal with this problem and the factionalism which helped to cause it, a number of measures were taken. First, party leadership at enterprise level was greatly strengthened. Secondly, efforts were made to draft new "rational rules and regulations" for management which were said to be significantly different from those which pertained in 1965. Thirdly, these rules were accompanied by a tighter system of accounting which was to encourage sound business procedure without "putting profits in command." Fourthly, attempts were made to encourage cadres to take part in collective manual labor and workers to take greater responsibility in management. Fifthly, a moderate wage reform was carried out which raised the average wage by about 10 per cent. Finally, welfare expenditures were greatly increased and occasionally reached 36 per cent of the wage bill.

RURAL INCENTIVES AND RURAL COMMERCE

While labor discipline in rural areas remained largely unaffected by the Cultural Revolution, and the restructuring of leadership at the commune level and below was not much more than a matter of formality, the question of "rational incentives" was nonetheless an important one. In the Constitution, adopted in January 1975 at the Fourth National People's Congress, it was made clear that certain concessions to peasant thrift were to remain: private plots, individual sideline production and private ownership of livestock in pastoral areas were to be permitted. In institutionalizing the people's communes, moreover, the Constitution also protected the accounting rights of production teams. Since a draft of the Constitution had been presented to the Second Plenum of the Ninth Central Committee in 1970, and since the sections of this draft which dealt with the rural sector were largely retained, it seems safe to conclude that rural policy was quite well defined by the end of 1970.[14]

The priority attached to the development of agriculture and the channelling of industrial output to support it certainly helped to raise the income of the communes and, therefore, of the peasants. Relaxation of restrictions on sideline production and the development of rural industries naturally also contributed to increasing rural income. Likewise, the greater concern given to the rural sector by commercial departments and the restructuring of the rural commercial network were of significant importance to the support of agriculture and improvement in rural living standards.

The strengthening of the rural commercial network was mainly reflected in the reliance on representatives of poor and lower-middle class peasants to run rural commercial co-operatives and the expansion of the commercial network into the remote communes and brigades. The aim was to provide a better service, but this was not to be limited merely to an increase in the amount of goods. It also included new supply schedules and the provision of a greater variety of products suitable for local needs. The expansion of sideline production in rural areas naturally implied that rural demands would become increasingly complex and that more sophisticated purchasing plans would have to be devised to absorb these sideline products. The rural commercial network even extended its service to providing advice on the proper handling of the relationship between grain production and sideline production, the local accumulation of investment funds, the introduction of new agricultural inputs and new technology, and the training of technical personnel.

FOREIGN TRADE

China's foreign trade showed a slight reduction in 1967 and 1968, but the second half of 1968 already witnessed a marked recovery.[15] It may be noted

---

[14] According to intelligence sources in Taipei, a draft of the Constitution of the People's Republic of China was passed at the second plenum of the Ninth Central Committee of the Communist Party of China in September 1970. For the text of the draft Constitution obtained by the sources, see Liu Ch'ing-po (Simpson C. P. Liu), *Zhonggong Xianfa Lun* [A Review of the Constitution of the People's Republic of China] (published by author, Taipei, 1973), pp. 427–436.

[15] For statistics on China's foreign trade, see Chen Nai-ruenn, "China's Foreign Trade,

that a sharp deterioration in China's exports to Hong Kong in these two years was a major reason for the relatively poor trade performance; China's overall trade pattern was, in fact, not much affected. On the whole, it did not appear that the Cultural Revolution had any significant impact on China's trade policy.

Apparently, China's foreign trade increased rapidly after the cultural Revolution from US$3,860 million in 1969 to US$14,090 million in 1975.[16] With the notable exceptions of 1974 and 1975 in which very considerable trade deficits were incurred, China roughly maintained a balance in its annual trade accounts. The expansion in trade was due to the increasing capacity to export rice, textiles, handicrafts and petroleum, and the intent was to import foreign plants and technology to speed up economic development. Success in establishing trade relations with practically every part of the world obviously also contributed to this expansion, though China's major trading partners remained more or less the same as in the 1960s, with the United States being the only new partner of any significance.

The most interesting aspect of China's foreign trade, as far as development strategy was concerned, was perhaps the acquisition and diffusion of advanced foreign technology. Since 1970, the Chinese leaders looked outwards once again for the acquisition of capital equipment and know-how on a substantial scale. They purchased large numbers of complete plants to increase output in a number of basic industries, primary metallurgy, petro-chemicals and energy. From December 1972 to the spring of 1975, contracts worth between US$2.2 and 2.5 billion were made, principally with Japan, France and West Germany, with deliveries extending through 1977.[17] Imports of plants and technology, therefore, rose more rapidly in these years than in any previous period.

How should this large-scale import of foreign plants and technology be evaluated? The significance or the "weight" of this technological import in the Chinese development strategy and the problems associated with its unprecedented scale surely merit attention. There is no doubt that the principle of self-reliance continued to be stressed with at least three objectives in view: (1) to minimize China's strategic and financial dependence on foreign countries; (2) to create a self-confident generation of Chinese and guard against contamination by foreign influences; and (3) to mobilize local savings

---

1950–74," in *China: A Reassessment of the Economy. A Compendium of Papers Submitted to the Joint Economic Committee, Congress of the U. S.* (Washington, D. C.: Government Printing Office, 1975), p. 645. On the recovery in the second half of 1968, see *Far Eastern Economic Review Yearbook: Asia 1970*, p. 107.

[16] Chen Nai-ruenn, *op. cit.*; and *Far Eastern Economic Review Yearbook: Asia 1977*, p. 159.

[17] Alexander Eckstein, "China's Trade Policy and Sino-American Relations," *Foreign Affairs*, Vol. 54, No. 1 (October 1975), p. 140.

so as to economize on scarce foreign exchange and state investment funds. The pursuit of self-reliance in these terms in past decades in fact enabled the Chinese to achieve a high degree of technical and economic independence.

It may also be noted that, throughout the history of the People's Republic of China (up to 1976), foreign trade lagged behind economic growth so that the Chinese economy was actually becoming less oriented to foreign trade. According to Alexander Eckstein, trade as a proportion of GNP dropped from an estimated 8 per cent in the 1950s to perhaps around 5 per cent in the mid-1970s.[18] Even if this ratio were to be maintained in the near future, which appears unlikely since the fall of the Gang of Four, the import of foreign technology would still increase due to changes in the composition of imports. As the newly imported plants gradually come into operation, the output of chemical fertilizers and steel may be expected to increase dramatically. Thus, when China achieves a greater degree of self-sufficiency not only in grain but also in these two items, a much larger amount of foreign currency will become available for further technological imports. In fact, the increase in such imports in this period (1952-76) reflected China's increased import capacity rather than a deliberate change in policy in favor of foreign plants and technology. After all, China had looked to the West for such imports ever since the early 1960s.

In Chinese industry as a whole, the highly structured process of internal diffusion certainly appeared to be a more important source of technological advancement than the technology acquired from abroad. The Chinese leadership, moreover, seemed willing to accept some short-term retardation of growth in order, in the long run, to attain the social goals of mass participation and self-reliance. In an economy which "walks on two legs," the major task was surely to raise the technological level of the farm machinery repair shops in the county to that of the tractor plants in Shenyang. In qualitative terms, however, imports of technology would still be an important factor in the development of the more sophisticated sectors of Chinese industry. In some areas, outputs based on inefficient and obsolescent plants could be dramatically improved by the importation of modern technology and production facilities, as in the case of Rolls Royce Spey engines.[19] Imports of technology, and the industrial exhibitions which went along with them, provided valuable international scientific contacts and information. These exhibitions provided good opportunities for purchasing display models at favorable prices for the purpose of analysis and copying. Programs for the importation of complete plants often included also the training of Chinese personnel by foreign firms. The construction of the large steel complex in Wuhan, jointly installed by

[18] *Ibid.*, pp. 138-139.
[19] *The Times* (London), December 17, 1975, p. 6.

DEMAG and Nippon Steel, for example, provided a six-month training course in Japan for Chinese technical personnel.[20] Thus, the existence of a highly skilled pool of technical manpower would help the Chinese assimilate sophisticated technology.

As may be expected, the considerable increase in China's foreign trade and imports of foreign plants and technology—at least in absolute terms—posed serious problems and political dilemas. China's increased involvement in the international economy exposed it somewhat to the uncertainties of the world market, as was clearly demonstrated in 1974. The global recession and double-digit inflation caused Chinese exports to suffer from both a decline in demand and a deterioration in the terms of trade. Since a sizeable share of Chinese imports were based on advance commitments, China incurred huge deficits in 1974 and 1975, amounting to about US$1.1 billion and 400 million respectively.[21] In order to finance this trade gap, the principle of "self reliance" was stretched to dangerous limits.

The Chinese leadership's concern for self-reliance finally resulted in the employment of a number of devices either to defer payment for goods received or to obtain foreign exchange to pay for them. These ranged from quite short-term 30-day suppliers' credits to 5-year deferred-payment schemes linked to complete plant deliveries. In addition, a number of West European and Japanese banks were invited to place foreign currency deposits in the Bank of China at Eurodollar rates (or at rates approximating these) for periods of up to one year, and renewable annually. These deposits might have amounted to several hundred million dollars in 1974, and they could be considered as loans in disguise.[22] Moreover, the large-scale influx of Western visitors also meant greater exposure of Chinese managers and technicians to capitalist ways, a greater acceptance of foreign expertise and technology to Chinese development, and, therefore, a greater threat of back-sliding into a "slavish comprador philosophy" and "revisionism." So it is small wonder that in the campaign to criticize Lin Piao and Confucius in 1972-74, foreign technology was a hotly-debated issue and the Chinese were warned against the evil Liu Shao-ch'i/Lin Piao "revisionist" line of "worshipping foreign things."

DISCUSSION AND CONCLUSION

In the evolution of the Chinese development strategy, the proper handling of the relationships between industry and agriculture, between industry in the

[20] Alexander Eckstein, *op. cit.*, p. 145.

[21] Chen Nai-ruenn, *op. cit.*; *Far Eastern Economic Review Yearbook: Asia 1976*, p. 153; and Alexander Eckstein, *op. cit.*, pp. 147-148.

[22] Alexander Eckstein, *op. cit.*, p. 149.

coastal regions and industry in the interior, between the state, the units of production and the individual producers, etc., was at least as important as economic growth. The assurance of a minimum standard of living and the narrowing of income inequalities are stated objectives of economic programs in most developing countries. These objectives, together with the preservation of socialist values, were assigned a high priority in deed as well as in word.

Though a contentious point, many would agree that the experiments with an original Chinese development strategy embodied in the Great Leap Forward ended almost in economic disaster. The direction of economic policy after the Cultural Revolution, however, suggested some kind of synthesis of elements of the Great Leap and concessions to the materialistic demands of peasants and workers. The groundwork for this new course seemed to have been laid and management of the economy appeared more decentralized, with considerable emphasis on the development of small-scale rural industry.

In the agricultural sector, the continued improvement of the water control system and the general increase in agricultural inputs constituted key elements in the long-term upward trend of farm output. Though many water control projects were only partly finished and major rivers and large tributaries remained to be harnessed, irrigation and water control in the more distant future would surely show diminishing returns. Mechanization, chemical fertilizers and improved seeds, on the other hand, would assume increasing importance. Hua Kuo-feng's report to the First National Conference on Learning from Tachai appeared to have demonstrated this awareness.[23] Chinese agriculture also benefited from the broadening of education and training in rural areas, the increased experience of the work force with fertilizers and machinery, and the assignment to the countryside since 1968 of nearly 10 million secondary school graduates from urban areas.[24] The policy of "walking on two legs" continued to satisfy short-term and long-term rural requirements. For example, simple seed selection and crossing were practiced by peasants, and limited scientific capabilities were devoted to sophisticated varietal development. The problem, of course, was to ensure that these activities would complement rather than hinder each other. Similar problems existed in rural industries, and guidelines were needed.

According to Eckstein's estimates, only 28 per cent of China's national product in 1970 derived from agriculture, as compared with 45 per cent in 1952.[25]

[23]For excerpts of the report in English, see *Peking Review*, Vol. 18, No. 44 (October 31, 1975), pp. 7-10 and 18.

[24]Arthur G. Ashbrook Jr., "China: Economic Review, 1975," in *China: A Reassessment of the Economy*, p. 30.

[25]Alexander Eckstein, "Economic Growth and Change in China: A Twenty-Year Perspective," *The China Quarterly*, No. 54 (April-June 1973), p. 236.

The agricultural sector was, therefore, of diminishing significance in China's economic development, and the emphasis on the agricultural sector in the Chinese development strategy was largely based on social and political factors. If Chinese leaders had not adopted the policy of deliberately favoring the rural sector, the country would almost certainly have developed a dual economy. The problem certainly was still far from solved. Although agricultural output had been increasing steadily since 1962, its growth rate was vastly outstripped by that of industry. There was no indication that the proportion of the total work-force engaged in agriculture (75 per cent) had diminished, and the migration of secondary school graduates from urban to rural areas continued to be strongly encouraged. The development of rural industries and the increase in supply of modern inputs from the industrial sector were, of course, aimed at eliminating the very considerable differences in living standards between the two sectors; fiscal means were also adopted to improve the terms of trade for peasants. Using 1952 prices as base figures, Nicholas Lardy has estimated that, between 1952 and 1974, the prices of farm products paid by the state increased by 64.4 per cent while prices of industrial goods sold in rural areas increased by a mere 0.3 per cent.[26] These fiscal measures achieved fast results, but ultimately they depended on the amount of resources devoted to the support of the rural sector.

It is of interest to note that much of the tremendous increase in contracts for Western industrial plants in 1973 and 1974 (US$1.2 billion in 1973 and $850 million in 1974, compared with only $60 million in 1972) was not designed to increase the machine-building or mining capacity but rather to expand several-fold the capacity to produce chemical fertilizers and artificial fibers.[27] Between November 1972 and May 1974, China bought 13 large urea plants from Japan, Western Europe and the United States at a total cost of US$500 million.[28] Output from these plants, if supplemented by improved water control facilities and increased supplies of other types of fertilizers, should boost agricultural output considerably by 1980 and the need for imports of grain and nitrogen fertilizers might be eliminated, even in poor crop years. The amount of foreign exchange spent was surely a good indication of the Chinese leadership's determination to tackle the problems of the rural sector.

Performance in the industrial sector was satisfactory in the post-Cultural Revolution period, as confirmed by the figures released by Premier Chou in early 1975.[29] The policy of supporting agriculture in the past years, as analyzed

[26] Nicholas R. Lardy, "Economic Planning and Income Distribution in China," *Current Scene*, Vol. 14, No. 11 (November 1976), p. 6.

[27] Arthur G. Ashbrook Jr., *op. cit.*, p. 31.

[28] *Ibid.*, p. 29.

[29] Chou En-lai, "Report on the Work of the Government," *op. cit.*

above, probably set the stage for a break-through in agriculture in the early 1980s and this break-through, in turn, could boost industrial production. In the first place, the increased production of agricultural raw materials could provide more inputs for light industry. Secondly, the foreign exchange currently needed to purchase grain and fertilizers could be freed for industrial investment.

More balanced efforts to promote growth would be required so as to correct the existing structural flaws in industry. The shortages of electric power, coal, iron ore, etc., in the 1970s reflected fundamental imbalances in extractive, processing and finishing industries. In metallurgy, for example, investment was concentrated too heavily on the development of crude steel capacity at the expense of mining and finished steel.

To deal with the unbalanced distribution of industries, the Chinese undertook a deliberately phased policy of regional development beginning with the First Five-Year Plan. The specific provisions governing the geographical distribution of industrial capital construction were as follows: (1) expansion of existing industrial bases, especially in north east China, in order to support the construction of new industrial areas; (2) construction of new industrial bases in north China and central China, centering around two new iron and steel complexes to be built in Paotow and Wuhan; and (3) the construction of a new industrial base in south west China. According to the rates of provincial industrial growth between 1949 and 1974, provided by Nicholas Lardy, many of the least-industrialized interior regions of China, such as Kansu, Tsinghai, Ninghsia and Inner Mongolia, actually sustained the highest rates of growth.[30] On the other hand, many of the provinces which were highly developed in 1949 grew relatively slowly. China's leading industrial center, Shanghai, for example, was one of the slowest growing areas. South west China seemed to have lagged slightly behind; though it also appeared likely that the investments in the infrastructure in that region in the first half of the 1970s, particularly in the transportation sector (symbolized by the completion of the Chengtu-Kunming railway), would start to pay off in the near future.

Since the early 1970s, there had been a series of small improvements in the quality, variety and availability of consumer goods; and the extent of improvement was probably most noticeable in the ownership of consumer durables— bicycles, watches, transistor radios, cameras, and sewing machines. This phenomenon reflected the amount of resources devoted to light industries. Such commodities, however, were still largely available only to industrial workers and to members to well-to-do communes. The problem, therefore, was whether the increasing availability of such commodities at cheaper prices

[30]Nicholas R. Lardy, *op. cit.*, pp. 10-11.

would, in fact, aggravate real income differentials. In many ways, this might well be a temporary and necessary evil since the expansion of consumer goods industries would most probably be a lengthy process.

Finally, any discussion of China's development strategy must also consider population growth. Estimates of the Chinese population in the mid-1970s ranged from 800 to 920 million. The population control program, which was much more vigorous than the campaigns of 1956-58 and 1962-66, was only in operation since the Cultural Revolution and only just began to take effect in the rural areas. Although its importance was appreciated, cadres at all levels probably had a host of other programs competing for their attention. If the highest priority were to be given to curbing the birth rate in the next decade, the Chinese would have the organization, the technology and a changing social climate to make the program a success. Indeed, some encouraging signs emerged in early 1977. It was revealed that in Hopei and Kiangsu, the population growth rate had declined from 25 per thousand in 1965 to around 10 per thousand, and Shanghai and Peking had managed to keep their population growth to below 6 per thousand.[31] The major task in the future would be to bring the rates in the rural areas down to the level of those in Peking and Shanghai.

In this general survey of the Chinese development strategy in the post-Cultural Revolution period, the significance of the purge of Lin Piao, the campaign to criticize Lin Piao and Confucius, the campaign to study the theory of the Dictatorship of the Proletariat, the criticisms of Teng Hsiao-p'ing, and the arrest of the Gang of Four have all been conspicuously neglected. An easy way out is to say that the scope of the chapter does not allow a detailed analysis of the impact of these events. Also, the broad outline of the development strategy discussed above appeared to have been confirmed both at the Tenth Party Congress in August 1973 and at the Fourth National People's Congress in January 1975. Thus, throughout this period, the Chinese development strategy did not seem to have been substantially affected by such crises, although the expansion of trade and the introduction of foreign plants and technology, which stretched the self-reliance principle to its very limits in the mid-1970s, especially in the field of foreign credit, did give cause for criticism. The Gang of Four in fact never succeeded in formulating any credible alternative to replace this development strategy.

Yet, what caused the apparently abrupt changes in this development strategy made by the present Chinese leadership after the fall of the Gang of

---

[31] "Family Planning," *Peking Review*, Vol. 20, No. 13 (March 25, 1977), p. 29.

Four?[32] The basic cause seems to be that the present leadership recognized that the molding of a new generation of socialist men and women requires a certain material base which should come first in time. To accelerate the building of this material base, the leadership was prepared to introduce foreign capital and technology, to relax the principle of self-reliance, and to use material incentives to boost production. In 1956, it was agreed at the Eighth Party Congress that the most important contradiction in the domestic scene was that between an advanced system of relationships in production and the backward forces of production.[33] The obvious solution was to promote economic growth and increase productivity so as to resolve the contradiction. The Maoists, however, believed that this would not be adequate because the concentration of efforts on economic growth and increase in productivity would endanger the very existence of the advanced system of relationships in production which would then probably back-slide into "revisionism." A Cultural Revolution became necessary not only because it would help eliminate this danger, but also because it would produce a push from the superstructure to help promote economic growth and increase productivity. Unfortunately, the Cultural Revolution launched by Chairman Mao and his supporters in 1966-69 not only failed to produce this superstructural push, but it also led to political chaos and decline in production, though it did make the Chinese much more aware of the dangers of a Soviet type of socialism or "revisionism." The vast majority of Chinese and the present Chinese leadership seem to believe that such a price was too high.

Viewed from another angle, the Chinese development strategy discussed

[32] For a general outline of the new development strategy adopted by the present Chinese leadership and the adjustments made subsequently, see the following important policy documents: (a) "Unite and Strive to Build a Modern, Powerful Socialist Country!", Premier Hua Kuo-feng's report on the work of the government delivered at the first session of the Fifth National People's Congress on February 26, 1978, *Peking Review*, Vol. 21, No. 10 (March 10, 1978), pp. 7-40, especially pp. 18-26; (b) Communique of the third plenary session of the 11th Central Committee of the Communist Party of China adopted on December 22, 1978, *ibid.*, Vol. 21, No. 52 (December 29, 1978), pp. 6-16, especially pp. 11-13; (c) Premier Hua Kuo-feng's report on the work of the government delivered at the second session of the Fifth National People's Congress on June 18, 1979, *ibid.*, Vol. 22, No. 27 (July 6, 1979), pp. 5-31, especially pp. 11-21; (d) Communique of the fourth plenary session of the 11th Central Committee of the Communist Party of China adopted on September 28, 1979, *ibid.*, Vol. 22, No. 40 (October 5, 1979), pp. 32-34.

[33] This decision of the Eighth Party Congress was condemned as revisionist during the Cultural Revolution, but has recently been reaffirmed; see Yeh Chien-ying's speech at the meeting on September 29, 1979, in celebration of the 30th anniversary of the founding of the People's Republic of China, *Peking Review*, Vol. 22, No. 40 (October 5, 1979), pp. 7-32, especially p. 13.

above clearly placed certain socialist values above absolute economic growth, and the Chinese leadership then was quite prepared to sacrifice pure economic growth in the pursuit of such values. It was exactly this pursuit which won so much admiration from the radicals as well as the liberals in the West, and it was exactly this pursuit which enabled the Chinese to claim that they had an alternative and indeed superior development strategy to offer to the Third World. Yet these long-term values gradually became meaningless to the masses in the absence of substantial improvement in the Chinese living standard, and the lower living standard cast doubt upon the superiority of the socialist system. The political chaos and injustice which became prevalent during and after the Cultural Revolution further disillusioned the Chinese who then began to question the wisdom of this sacrifice of economic growth. To cite the extreme, the path followed by Japan, and later by South Korea, Taiwan, Singapore and Hong Kong surely presents a more attractive model to the Third World in the late 1970s than the Chinese road to socialism.

The present Chinese leadership now concentrates on the attempt to accomplish the comprehensive modernization of agriculture, industry, national defense and science and technology before the end of the century. This grandiose goal is certainly respectable in itself, but it is almost impossible for the present Chinese leadership to avoid the basic issues or contradictions considered in this chapter. How does one try to achieve balanced sectoral growth and egalitarian distribution in the economy while making allowances for policies of imbalance which might release human creativity? How does one resolve the contradiction between increasing demands for consumption and investment? How does one profit from foreign trade and not be subject to the crises of the capitalist world? How does one import advanced technology from the West but not the inbuilt capitalist relations? The achievement of the "four modernizations" does not need to include a satisfactory resolution of the above contradictions, yet a resolution is desirable. Most probably it requires a combination of pragmatism and idealism to re-establish the Chinese road to socialism as an alternative and indeed superior development model for the Third World.

CHAPTER SEVEN

In Defense of Bureaucracy: The De-radicalization of Maoism

Ambrose Yeo-chi King

The downfall of the Gang of Four is a turning point in Chinese communist history. Its significance at both the symbolic and practical level is as great as that of the Great Proletarian Cultural Revolution, but these two stand out as the thesis versus anti-thesis in the dialectical and historical process. The dramatic effect of the fall of Chiang Ch'ing, Yao Wen-yuan, Chang Ch'un-chiao and Wang Hung-wen can only be equaled by that of the third political come-back of Teng Hsiao-p'ing. This incredible political story is still in the process of developing. However, if the present developmental pattern and direction continue unchanged, then a thorough and far-reaching de-radicalization of Maoism will inevitably change the face of the Chinese continent. A de-radicalization process of Maoism is taking place on a large scale and in a systematic way on all fronts of the Chinese system, including science and technology, education, economy, literature and the arts. This de-radicalizing movement, which has a heavy pragmatic bent, is carried out with great fanfare under the banner of the so-called "Four Modernizations" which were acclaimed by Chou En-lai, former Premier, prior to his untimely death.[1] The purpose of this chapter is not to give a detailed analysis of the dimensions of the de-radicalization of Maoism, but only to concentrate on the most outstanding pheno-menon of this movement, that is, a return to modernization and bureaucracy.

After the outbreak of the Cultural Revolution in 1966 a rather systematic anti-bureaucratic ideology developed which is now under systematic criticism and repudiation. Anti-bureaucratism is the legacy of the Cultural Revolution

---

[1] The Four Modernizations Program was announced by Chou En-lai at the Second Session of the Central Committee of the Tenth Party Congress and the First Session of the Fourth National People's Congress. Based on this grandiose program, Communist China attempts to transform her developing socialist society into an advanced modernized society on a par with the most modernized societies of the world before the end of this century. The original idea of making China a strong socialist modernized society within a short time span was suggested by Mao in 1963.

which has enjoyed the most significant appeal, but after the fall of the Four a "new" ideology defending the bureaucratic system has emerged. The anti-bureaucratism of the Cultural Revolution was intended to combat the alleged de-radicalizing tendency of Liu Shao-ch'i or, using the communist jargon, to "struggle against revisionism," or to prevent a "change of color" of the revolution. This movement was manifested most violently in the form of attacking the Party and State machineries. In their places emerged a charismatic leader and mass activism tainted with violence, rebellion and disorder. As of now, under the overriding objective of modernization, the attack on the Four signifies nothing less than combating the radicalizing tendency of the Cultural Revolution. Again to use the Chinese communist jargon, it is intended to build "great stability" and "great order" and to protect the socialist construction of China.[2] This counter-movement is most vividly manifested in its ideological reemphasis on party-building and state-building in which authority and discipline are emphatically stressed.

MAOISM AS AN IDEOLOGY OF MODERNIZATION

Maoism during the Cultural Revolution period reached its peak as an ideological system and it is now still the governing ideology of China. However, since Mao's death, Maoism has become what Bertram Wolfe has said about Marxism, a "multiple ambiguity." To rephrase Wolfe's words slightly, "it is because of ambiguity in the spirit of Mao himself, ambiguity in the heritage he left, and ambiguity in those who claimed to be his heirs."[3] During the period of the Cultural Revolution, Chinese communist propaganda, which was then controlled by the Four, articulated a version of Maoism emphasizing revolutionary romanticism and voluntaristic mass spontaneity and activism, which has now been repudiated as a "sham" Maoism. Today, Maoism has been given a new formal definition. Thanks to the "ambiguity" of the thought of Mao Tse-tung, Maoism has been rightly or wrongly reinterpreted and redefined

[2] Hua Kuo-feng publicly advocates the theme of order and stability, and uses Mao's words to legitimize his firm stand on it. Mao is quoted to have said: "Great disorder across the land leads to great order" and "Eight years have passed since the Great Proletarian Cultural Revolution started. It is preferable to have stability now." See Hua's "Political Report to the Eleventh National Congress of the Communist Party" in *The Eleventh National Congress of the Communist Party of China (Documents)* (Peking: Foreign Languages Press, 1977), pp. 51-53.

[3] The "multiple ambiguity" of Marxism results from, says Bertram Wolfe, "ambiguity in the spirit of Marx himself, ambiguity in the heritage he left, and ambiguity in those who claimed to be his heirs." Quoted in M. M. Drachkovitch (ed.), *Marxist Ideology in the Contemporary World—Its Appeals and Paradoxes* (New York: Frederick A. Prager, 1966), p. xii.

as an ideology of economic construction and development of productivity. This newly defined interpretation of Maoism becomes nothing but an ideology of "socialist" modernization. At this juncture, it should be understood that the so-called Maoism is a Chinese version of Marxism and, more specifically, Mao's version of Marxism-Leninism. Before Mao's death, Maoism was what Mao himself verified, which was sometimes inconsistent in emphasis, if not in substance. However, with the departure of the charismatic leader, the official version of Maoism can only be defined by the men in power at given periods of time. Maoism has become an "institutional" Maoism par excellence, to borrow Kolakowski's expression.[4] Fortunately, it is not the concern of this chapter to decide what is authentic or sham Maoism. What we can say with certainty is that there are at least two Maoisms, Radical Maoism and Modernistic Maoism, in the Chinese communist history since 1949. The two Maoisms, claiming with equal force to be Mao's heirs and to carry out the heritage of the charismatic leader, are clearly shown during the Cultural Revolution and in the post-Cultural Revolution stage respectively. The post-Cultural Revolution's Modernistic Maoism has taken a subtle ideological twist to protect the integrity of Mao on the one hand, and to discredit the radical elements of Maoism on the other. It is necessary to protect the integrity of Mao because Mao's charisma is still the legitimate source for Hua Kuo-feng and the modernistic elites (Hua's "unchallengeable status" as leader derived from Mao's statement "with you in charge, I am at ease"). It is also a necessity to discredit Radical Maoism in order to salvage the goal of modernization and socialist construction from the wreckage of anarchistic rule. This ideological twist is vividly, though ironically, expressed in Hua's statement delivered at the Eleventh National Congress of the Party which reads:

> Now that the Gang has been overthrown, we are able to achieve stability and unity and attain great order across the land in compliance with Chairman Mao's instruction. Thus, the smashing of the Gang of Four marks the triumphant conclusion of our first Great Proletarian Cultural Revolution, which lasted eleven years.[5]

In a word, a drastic change in the goal structure of Maoism is made through the very emphasis on the integrity of Mao and his ideological system. Indeed, it is "a change carried on beneath symbols of nonchange," which typifies the

---

[4] "Institutional" Maoism here means a doctrine defined purely, formally, its contents being in every case supplied by the decree of the infallible institution, be it a charismatic leader or a charismatic Party. The distinction between intellectual Marxism and institutional Marxism is brilliantly analyzed by Leszek Kolakowski in his *Marxism and Beyond* (London: Paladin, 1968; trans. by Jane Zielonko Peel), pp. 191 ff.

[5] *The Eleventh National Congress of the Communist Party of China (Documents)*, p. 52.

latent process of de-radicalization.[6] The new post-Cultural Revolution ideology makes it crystal clear that the modernization of China is the overriding goal of the Chinese communist revolution. It emphasizes the importance of economic construction, the importance of building up the material bases. A theory of materialist reflection has been forcefully reemphasized as the paradigm for a genuine Chinese Marxism. Nowhere is this more clear than in the following statement:

> Marxism holds that, within the contradictions between the productive forces and the relations of production, between practice and theory, and between the economic base and the superstructure, the productive forces, practice, and the economic base generally play the principal and decisive role. Whoever denies this is not a materialist.[7]

Reading this statement, we cannot help being reminded of the "scientific" version of Marxism.[8] The touchstone distinguishing authentic and sham Marxism or authentic and sham Maoism is now solely according to the new interpretation: whether or not it will contribute to the development of the

[6] Yinger writes, "Religious change is usually a latent process, carried on beneath symbols of nonchange." (See J. Milton Yinger, *Sociology Looks at Religion* [New York: Macmillan, 1963], p. 70.) Robert Tucker believes what Yinger has written of religious change can also be applied to ideological movements of radical persuasion. He further writes, "Not the end of ideology but rather the growth of a stable discrepancy between ideological symbols and political deeds is the true mark of de-radicalizing change in once-radical movements." See R. C. Tucker, *The Marxian Revolutionary Idea* (London: George Allen and Unwin, 1970), p. 214.

[7] This statement is quoted from "On the General Program for the Whole Party and the Whole Nation," one of the famous "Three Documents" written under the auspices of Teng Hsiao-p'ing. The other two are: "Some Problems in Accelerating Industrial Development" and "On Some Problems in the Fields of Science and Technology." It should be pointed out that these three documents, once viciously attacked by the Four as "three poisonous weeds," are now praised as "three fragrant flowers." The total reversal of the verdict on the "three poisonous weeds" appeared in *People's Daily* on June 30, July 8 and July 16, 1977 respectively. All the criticizing-the-Four literature pouring out in the post-Four period is basically nothing but further elaboration of the views contained in the "three fragrant flowers." Therefore, the "three fragrant flowers" may be viewed as the modernistic elites' paradigm for Chinese socialist development. Please see Chi Hsin, *The Case of the Gang of Four: With First Translation of Teng Hsiao-P'ing's "Three Poisonous Weeds"* (Hereafter referred to as Teng's Documents) (Hong Kong: Cosmos Books, 1977), p. 221.

[8] The "scientific" version of Marxism here refers to the theoretical stance that places "greatest reliance on the development of the forces of production, and on the opportunities and contradictions this will create." Contrary to this version of Marxism, the "critical" or Hegelian version of Marxism places its theoretical stress on consciousness and superstructures. A stimulating and perceptive articulation of these two versions of Marxism can be found in "The Two Marxisms" in A. W. Gouldner, *For Sociology* (Harmondsworth: Penguin Books, 1975), pp. 425-462.

"economic situation" and productive forces.[9] It can be clearly seen that productive force is now recognized as having fundamental importance in dialectical Marxism, and Mao's creed has been changed from a story of salvation in the language of politics and revolution into a story of salvation in the language of economics and modernization. Before Mao's death, whether the emphasis was placed on "grasping revolution" or on "uplifting productivity" constituted, in essence, the struggle of "two lines." Radical Maoism, placing more emphasis on revolution, which was the "correct line" before the Fall of Four, is now repudiated as the "revisionist line." The capital crime Radical Maoists committed, it is alleged, was their conspiracy to thwart the nation's program of socialist modernization.[10] The Radical Maoists, who are accused of having aimed at the destruction of productivity, are alleged to have spread false "theories" as follows:

1. The theory of the natural development of productivity: The Gang of Four are quoted as saying, "once revolution is grasped, production will increase naturally and without spending any effort." This is now being criticized as a metaphysical theory which distorted and exaggerated Marxist dialecticalism to a ridiculous degree.[11] The present theory argues that production will not come "naturally," and revolution alone is no guarantee of production.

2. The theory of the unimportance of productivity: The Four are quoted as making the statement that "it does not matter whether the factories produce or not, the line must be correct"; "it does not matter whether there is a harvest or not, the peasant masses must engage in class struggle"; "it is better to have socialist low speed than to have capitalist high speed." These views are now being criticized as a theory concerned only with superstructure and the transformation of the relationship of production, ignoring totally the importance of developing productive

---

[9] This view is expressed in Teng's Document, *op. cit.*, p. 227. So far the most systematic and theoretical treatment of this point can be found in Z. L. Lin and Yew Lin, *A Critique on the Gang of Four's Critique on "Economism"* (Peking: People's Press, 1978).

[10] The Gang of Four was allegedly opposed to the modernization program, believing that modernization would mean the restoration of capitalism. See Chi Wei, "How the 'Gang of Four' Opposed Socialist Modernization." *Peking Review*, March 11, 1977, pp. 6-9. This was further discussed in O. Edmund Clubb's "China after Mao," *Current History*, Vol. 73, No. 429, pp. 49-53, 86.

[11] "Thoroughly Criticize the Gang of Four's Crime of Destroying Revolution and Production" by the Great Critique Section of the National Construction Committee, *People's Daily*, No. 11, 1976. See also "One Great Piece of Evidence on the Gang of Four's Crime to Usurp Power of the Party" by the Great Critique Section of the First Engineering-Industrial Department, *Kuang Ming Daily*, Dec. 6, 1976.

forces.[12] And the communism advocated by the Four is repudiated as a "communism without material bases."[13]

3. The theory that fostering productivity is bound to lead to revisionism: Chang Ch'un-chiao, the theoretican of the Four, is quoted as saying, "the satellite goes to the sky, the red flag falls to the ground," that is, whoever works for production is bound to become a productionist, or a disciple of "economism," thereby leading to the incorrect line of revisionism. This theory is now being criticized for falsifying the dichotomy between revolution and production, thus committing the crime of one-sidedness and metaphysical nonsense.[14]

4. The theory of politics being everything: The Four and Lin Piao are alleged to have advocated a sort of panpoliticism, which unduly distorted and exaggerated the role of politics in the process of building socialism, as though believing that "politics can combat everything." This is now being criticized for wrongly separating economics from politics, and production from revolution, thus undermining the proper role of economics and production.[15]

5. The theory of substituting Marxism for natural science: The Four are alleged to have advocated a "theory of substitution" which says that so long as Marxism is grasped, the laws governing nature will be understood. There is now the criticism that despite the extreme importance of Marxism as a guide for revolution and construction, it cannot be used to understand the inner logic of nature which belongs to the proper field of natural science.[16] Modernization of science and technology, one of the Four Modernizations, can therefore only be achieved through scientific research and experiment.

All in all, Modernistic Maoism is placing great importance on modernization in general and productivity in particular.

Communist China now feels there is a great need to build up a vast "army

[12]"Chairman Mao's Educational Instruction Cannot Be Distorted: Criticizing One of Chang Chun-chiao's Ridiculous Theories" by the Great Critique Section of the Ministry of Education, *Kuang Ming Daily*, Nov. 23, 1976.

[13]"Four Modernizations and the Dictatorship of the Proletariat: Thoroughly Criticize the Gang of Four's Capital Crime of Opposing Four Modernizations" by the Great Critique Section of the First Engineering-Industrial Department, *People's Daily*, March 12, 1977.

[14]*Ibid*; also see Rén Píng, "A Gang That Is Harmful to the Nation and the People: Criticize the Gang of Four's Crime in Obstructing the Works of Grasping Revolution and Uplifting Production," *People's Daily*, Nov. 14, 1976.

[15]See Teng's Documents, *op. cit.*, pp. 222-223.

[16]"Rebutting Yao Wen-yuan's 'Theory of Substitution' " by the Theoretical Section of the Academy of Science, *People's Daily*, March 16, 1977.

of productive enterprise" in order to launch "a new great leap forward."
Mr. Yu Chiu-li, Vice-Premier, declared that the problem of the speed of industrialization is a problem of how the proletarian class is to defeat the capitalist
class, socialism to defeat capitalism, and it concerns the future and the destiny
of the nation.[17] Moreover, Teng Hsiao-ping and his followers even go so far as
to publicly denounce the sacred notion of egalitarianism which is the favorite
slogan of Radical Maoism. It is now proclaimed unequivocally that there is
the "necessity of the existence of disparity" and, perhaps more surprising,
that "egalitarianism is not only impossible now, it is also impossible in the
future."[18] This certainly reminds us of Stalin's contempt for egalitarianism.[19]
Clearly, modernistic elites, like Stalinists, are more concerned with Marx's
"kingdom of necessity" than with his dream of the "realm of liberty."[20] They
are now defending the legitimacy of "socialist" profit-making and the sanction
of material incentives in the form of a work points system.[21] It is therefore
not illegitimate to compare the Modernistic Maoist version of communism
with that of Stalin, which considers communism not as a system of radical
distribution of wealth, but a system of creation of wealth and productive
capacity.[22] Indeed, Modernistic Maoists have consciously or unconsciously
taken a view that the "superiority" of socialism over capitalism lies in its
ability to create a higher and faster rate of productivity and economic development. This is unmistakably expressed by Hua Kuo-feng. Hua Kuo-feng says,
"the purpose of revolution is to liberate productivity; one of the most important tasks of the dictatorship of the proletariat is to develop productivity

[17]"To Mobilize the Working Class of the Whole Party and the Whole Nation in
Struggling for the Promotion of Taching Type Enterprise," *Collected Documents on the
National Conference on Learning from Taching*, (Peking People Press, May 1977), p. 57.

[18]See Teng's Documents, *op. cit.*, p. 265.

[19]Stalin asserted in 1934, "Every Leninist knows (that is, if he is a real Leninist) that
equality in the sphere of requirements and individual life is a piece of reactionary petty-
bourgeois absurdity worthy of a primitive sect of ascetics, but not of a socialist society
organized on Marxian lines . . . equalization . . . , leveling the requirements and the
individual lives of the members of society . . . has nothing in common with Marxism, with
Leninism," Quoted in Robert V. Daniels, *The Nature of Communism* (New York: Vintage
Books, 1962), p. 63.

[20]G. Myrdal writes, "They (communists) thus created something very different from
Marx's dream of the 'realm of liberty' that would replace the 'kingdom of necessity' and
in which . . . the state would 'wither away' and the government of men would give way
to the 'administration of things'." The adjustment of the doctrine was clearly marked by
Lenin's famous assertion that "communism is Soviet power plus electricity." See Myrdal's
Asian Drama (New York: Pantheon, 1968), Vol. III, p. 1908.

[21]"The PRC's New Labor Organization and Management Policy," *Current Scene*,
Vol. 15, Nos. 11 & 12, pp. 20-23.

[22]Consult Robert V. Daniels' "The Chinese Revolution in Russian Perspective,"
World Politics, Vol. 13, No. 2 (January 1961), pp. 210-230.

fast. Implementing technological innovation and revolution is for the purpose of creating a higher rate of labor productivity than that of capitalism," and "in the field of economic development, the socialist system should demonstrate its superiority to that of capitalism."[23] This attitude toward socialism convinces us that socialism is indeed not the next stage of capitalism, but an alternative model to industrialization and modernization.[24] From the above analysis, it is amply clear that the Chinese version of Marxism or Maoism has now been given a new meaning and a new definition, that is, an ideology of modernization. We are not here arguing whether this is a truer version of Marxism or Maoism. But one thing is sure: Marxism has indeed a theory of modernization.[25] Maoism, according to Schwartz, is not without a modernistic version.[26] Therefore, the post-Cultural Revolution's Modernistic Maoism is not totally a new paradigm for Chinese Marxism. Ulam has argued that "anti-industrialism and the most absolute faith in industrialization are two interwoven themes of Marxism."[27] If this is true, then, Radical Maoism is definitely a radical version of "anti-industrialism" while Modernistic Maoism is all for "industrialization."

IN DEFENSE OF BUREAUCRACY

Since developing productive forces and material bases have been considered by Modernistic Maoists as the true mark of Maoism, it is no surprise to find that in the whole process of de-radicalization, order and organization have been conspicuously emphasized, particularly the concepts of authority and discipline. Radical Maoists' anti-bureaucratism is now being accused of being a conspiracy of the Four to attack leaders and cadres of revolutionary

[23] "To Mobilize the Working Class of the Whole Party and the Whole Nation in Struggling for the Promotion of Taching Type Enterprise," pp. 8, 14.

[24] The view that socialism is the competitor rather than the heir of capitalism is shared widely by scholars. See for example, Herbert Marcuse, *Soviet Marxism* (Harmondsworth: Penguin Books, 1971), p. 14; Irving L. Horowitz, *Three Worlds of Developments* (New York: Oxford University Press, 1966), pp. 366 ff.; and Talcott Parsons, "Communism and the West: The Sociology of the Conflict," in Amitai and Eva Etzioni (eds.), *Social Change* (New York: Basic Books, 1964), p. 394.

[25] Consult Robert C. Tucker, *The Marxian Revolutionary Idea*, pp. 92-129, and John Kautsky, *The Political Consequences of Modernization* (New York: Wiley, 1973), esp. pp. 237-251.

[26] B. I. Schwartz, "Modernization and the Maoist Vision: Some Reflections on Chinese Communist Goals," in his *Communism and China: Ideology in Flux* (New York: Atheneum, 1970), pp. 162-185.

[27] Adam B. Ulam, *The Unfinished Revolution* (New York: Vintage Books, 1960), p. 64.

experience in order to usurp power.[28] Furthermore, mass spontaneity and mass romantic activism are now condemned as nothing but anarchism, and the Radical Maoist obsession with conflict is being repudiated as nihilism.[29] During the Cultural Revolution, the role of the Party was replaced by Mao and his radical ideology. Now the words of Lenin, Engels and Mao have been skillfully used by modernistic elites to re-affirm the positive role of organization and, above all, the supreme role of the Party.[30] The most systematic statement put forward by Modernistic Maoists about the indispensability of organization can be found in the following statement:

> As production, science, and technology become more developed, the required system of regulations which reflects such developments becomes more tightly knit. . . . *Not only is this so in capitalist society, it is also the same in socialist society and will be the same in the future communist society.*[31]

It is here that the universal essence of organization is clearly spelled out. In other words, organization is defended as an indispensable instrument for whatever type of social system, be it capitalist or socialist. This viewpoint is definitely further away from Marx, who believes that under the socialist system bureaucracy becomes unnecessary, but closer to Weber, who unreservedly argues that bureaucracy is even more needed in socialist society than in the capitalist one,[32] and Michels, who insists that "socialism is not merely a problem in economy" but that "socialism is also an administrative problem."[33] Those believing that socialism does not need organization or believing that under socialism every worker knows how to rule the country are holding a simplistic view. Lenin once had such a naive attitude. However as soon as he realized it was illusionary, he dismissed it as "fairy tales."[34] True enough, Radical Maoists did not advocate the withering away of organization, but they did advocate a kind of organization which is anti-bureaucratic in nature, emphasizing mass spontaneity and subjective human will which in essence is

[28] See Chóng Lián, "The Gang of Four and the Trotskyists," *People's Daily*, January 27, 1977.

[29] See, for example, Cheng Háng-shéng, "A Discussion on Rampant Metaphysics," *Kuang Ming Daily*, March 29, 1977.

[30] Teng's Documents, *op. cit.*, p. 233.

[31] *Ibid.* (italics are mine), pp. 230-231.

[32] Raymond Aron, *Main Currents in Sociological Thought* (Harmondsworth: Penguin Books, 1970), Vol. 2, pp. 219-220, 267.

[33] Robert Michels, *Political Parties* (New York: Collier Books, 1962), p. 350.

[34] Lenin's extremely swift reversion from the radical soviet democratism of "State and Revolution" to the radical party authoritarianism of "What Is To Be Done" is discussed in Daniel Bell, *The End of Ideology* (New York: Collier Books, 1961), pp. 355-392. This problem is also touched on in Perry Anderson, *Considerations on Western Marxism* (London: Humanities Press, 1976), p. 116.

an ultra-voluntarist type of organization. There is no denying the fact that this type of organization does have its ideological appeal, but its workability as an instrumet for rational management and modernization is, to say the least, questionable.[35] As of now, the voluntarist model of organization is severely attacked. The Radical Maoists are being accused of spreading "idealism," "apriorism" and "subjectivism"; they are even criticized as failing to comprehend "the Marxist principle that existence determines consciousness."[36] The modernistic elites now unabashedly advocate the value of bureacratic organization. It is emphatically proposed that to develop the socialist economy, "a strict system of regulations must be set up" and "the designation of responsibility is a nucleus of all systems of regulations."[37] It is also made abundantly clear that "there must be someone responsible for every piece of work and for every position."[38] Even capitalist management is now being defended on the ground that, while some of its elements have a class nature, others do not; and even the long repudiated Taylorism or scientific management is now recognized as having high scientific achievement.[39] It is beyond doubt that the modernistic elites are making every possible effort to re-establish a rational organization for the purpose of carrying out the so-called "Four Modernizations." They are not only re-emphasizing the importance of hierarchical organization and discipline more than ever, but are also doing everything to re-institute the authority of the Party. Hua Kuo-feng has said:

> We must reaffirm the discipline of the Party, namely, (1) the individual is subordinate to the organization; (2) the minority is subordinate to the majority; (3) the lower level is subordinate to the higher level; (4) the entire Party is subordinate to the Central Committee.[40]

Moreover, it is said, "no person or organization is allowed to stand above the Party."[41] It seems to us the modernistic elites are geared to building up a Party charisma to replace the deceased charismatic leader. In a word, personal charisma is now in the process of being replaced by institutional charisma.

[35] Ambrose Yeo-chi King, "A Voluntarist Model of Organization: the Maoist Version and Its Critique," *The British Journal of Sociology*, Vol. 28, No. 3 (September 1977), pp. 363-374.
[36] "Four Modernizations and the Dictatorship of the Proletariat: Thoroughly Criticize the Gang of Four's Capital Crime of Opposing Four Modernizations."
[37] Teng's Documents, *op. cit.*, pp. 229-230.
[38] *Ibid.*
[39] "Bury Together with the Gang of Four the Big Stick of 'Control, Squeeze and Suppression'" by the Great Critique Section of the Petroleum Chemical-Industrial Department, *People's Daily*, February 15, 1977.
[40] *The Eleventh National Congress of the Comnunist Party of China (Documents)*, p. 104.
[41] Teng's Documents, *op. cit.*, p. 233.

In arguing for the need of organization or, more precisely, in defense of bureaucracy, modernistic elites have put forward a set of ideas as follows:

1. The need for hierarchy: It is argued that organization is not necessarily an instrument to "control, squeeze, suppress" the workers as Radical Maoists wrongly proposed.[42] The fashionable attitude of the Cultural Revolution, "go-against-the-tide," is condemned as responsible for chaos in management. Rebellion against authority is severely repudiated as is most clearly evidenced by the injunctions that students must respect their teachers.[43] The role of authority is defended by Engels' words: "wanting to abolish authority in large scale industry is tantamount to wanting to abolish industry itself, to destroying the power room in order to return to the spinning wheel."[44] The hierarchical organizational principle as mentioned above by Hua Kuo-feng is ferociously insisted upon.

2. The need for role specialization: While Radical Maoists attacked professionalism and role differentiation, the modernistic elites are arguing for a system of responsibility according to division of labor. It is said, "each cadre, worker, technician must be assigned a special job of responsibility," and "the key to any system of rules and regulations is to have a system of personal responsibility."[45]

3. The need for expertise: Expertness was viciously attacked by Radical Maoists during the Cultural Revolution and those giving emphasis to other than ideological motivation were accused of following the "white expert road." The modernistic elites are now arguing that having only ideology and political consciousness is not enough to be a good socialist man. An ideal socialist man must be a person with political consciousness plus technical and administrative skill, in a word, be both red and expert.[46] It is now stipulated that political meetings should be reduced and, for scientists and others, 5/6 time should be allocated for professional work.[47] While advocating both redness and expertness, in fact the

[42]*Ibid.*, pp. 229-230; also "Bury Together with the Gang of Four the Big Stick of 'Control, Squeeze and Suppression'."

[43]John Gardner, "Chou Jung-Hsin and Chinese Education," *Current Scene*, Vol. 15, Nos. 11 & 12, pp. 1-12.

[44]Teng's Documents, *op. cit.*, p. 230.

[45]*Ibid.*, pp. 251, 276.

[46]*Ibid.*, p. 268.

[47]The Radical Maoists believe that professionals divorced from manual work are bound to become a bureaucratic class. This view is at present being rebutted. It is argued now that work such as theoretical research should not be seen as being divorced from production and the revolutionary course. See Teng's Documents, *op. cit.*, p. 284; see also "The Notice Concerning the Convention on National Science Issued by the Central Committee of the Communist Party of China," *People's Daily*, September 23, 1977.

emphasis is being placed more and more on the latter.

4. The need for administrative rules: While Radical Maoists are alleged to have advocated the uselessness of institutions, it is argued now "a tight system of operational rules and job responsibility must be established."[48] The Taching's work attitude, the so-called "three honesty and four seriousness principles," is highly exalted.[49] Discipline is being more than ever emphasized, as discussed above. According to modernistic elites, "a struggle must be waged against attempts to violate the policy, the system, unified planning, fiscal and economic disciplines and work discipline."[50]

All the new concepts articulated above reveal that modernistic elites have unreservedly argued for the re-institution of bureaucratic organization, which was cursed during the Cultural Revolution. What the modernistic elites argue for is in fact a type of organization of a Weberian nature. Indeed, a case can be made that in the process of socialist modernization, a theoretical triumph goes to Weber rather than to Marx.

CONCLUSION

Marx's analysis of early capitalism is indeed first-rate. But what Marxism provides, as Hartz argues, is mainly a "negative picture of capitalism."[51] Marx is almost completely silent on how to "build" a socialist society. The Soviet Union under the leadership of Lenin, especially under Stalin, "found" a way. Stalin transformed backward Russia into a powerful industrialized state in no more than half a century. Indeed, the Soviet achievement was once universally admired in the early twenties, particularly for its striking speed of industrial development. However, the Soviet success shows only that there is an alternative road other than the Western one to industrialization and modernization, but it cannot be viewed as the next stage to capitalism. It has become in effect an authoritarian bureaucratic socialism. China's early development undoubtedly followed the Soviet model and a gigantic Stalinist system of bureaucracy was created by Mao and his one-time comrade Liu Shao-ch'i.[52] What the Chinese Great Proletarian Cultural Revolution stands for symbolically

[48] Teng's Documents, op. cit., p. 262.
[49] The "three honesty" principles are: be an honest person, speak honestly and work honestly; the "four seriousness" principles are: serious organization, requirements, discipline and attitude. See Teng's Documents, op. cit., p. 272.
[50] Ibid., p. 270.
[51] Louis Hartz, "Democracy: Image and Reality," in William N. Chambers and Robert H. Salisbury (eds.), Democracy Today (New York: Collier Books, 1962), pp. 25-44.
[52] Consult Victor Nee and James Peck, China's Uninterrupted Revolution (New York: Pantheon Books, 1975), pp. 332 ff.

is nothing but an alternative to the Soviet bureaucratic model in tackling the problem of transition to socialism. Its overriding emphasis was not on production or economic development but on attacking China's socialist bureaucratic tendency. The radical anti-bureaucratic Maoism indeed captivated, to a significant extent, the interest and even admiration of scholars in the West, Marxists and non-Marxists alike. At the ideological level, the Radical Maoist political-conflict approach to coping with the universal and generic problem of "means of administration" of Weber, rather than the specific and transient problem of "means of production" of Marx, can be viewed as an attractive way to arrest the recalcitrant force of bureaucracy. In actuality, however, the Radical Maoist anti-bureaucratic movement was not aimed at paving the road for the withering away of bureaucracy but was instead establishing a kind of primitive mass organization in order to replace the ruling bureaucratic apparatus. As a consequence, a nation-wide anarchistic tendency prevailed. Management in the fields of economics was especially damaged despite its symbolic significance. The Cultural Revolution made China bankrupt organizationally, culturally and economically. This in fact made Radical Maoists extremely unpopular. The Radical Maoists probably went beyond the limit of what the public mood could afford to tolerate and this might well be the reason why the shattering of the Four was achieved without shooting one bullet.

Today, the modernistic elites (of whom Teng Hsiao-p'ing is certainly the living symbol) have tried extremely hard to maintain the integrity of Mao in appearance by upholding Mao's thoughts emphasizing material development and institution-building. Their great effort is geared to a subtle transformation of Maoism into an ideology of modernization. This newly emerged Modernistic Maoism sanctions economic development and construction. The architectonic concept is productivity. And every effort has been made to increase productivity through re-institution of bureaucratic authority and discipline. The whole "criticizing Four" movement aims at reestablishing order for the purpose of strengthening the political and administrative apparatus. Bureaucracy of a Weberian kind is upheld as a rational instrument for the administration of things as well as of people. Indeed, what Lenin said, "ours is a workers' government with a bureaucratic twist"[53] can be equally applied to the present Chinese situation. The Chinese modernistic elites seem, like most Western organizational sociologists, to appreciate that bureaucracy is the most rational and effective organizational form for economic development and modernization.[54] They are now determined to get rid of all radical anti-bureaucratic

[53] Lenin, *Selected Works*, IX, 9, quoted in Daniel Bell, *The End of Ideology*, p. 383.

[54] It is interesting to know that some of those scholars who postulate the end of bureaucracy believe that "bureaucracy was a monumental discovery for harnessing the muscle power of the industrial revolution." See Warren G. Bennis, "Changing Organiza-

elements. The Leninist party concept and iron discipline are sternly upheld; important party leaders who were purged during the Cultural Revolution are coming back to power again.

All the events since the Four can only mean that the Cultural Revolution is fully repudiated. The historical period from 1949 to the eve of the Cultural Revolution, once condemned by Radical Maoists, is now re-recognized as a period of significant achievement in revolution and construction.[55] Maybe it is too dramatic a reversion for most students of China, but what Teng Hsiao-p'ing says, "without swinging a little further to the other extreme, the problem would not be resolved"[56] is not without reason. Realistically speaking, given China's economic backwardness, creation of wealth and the increase of productive capacity through a rational bureaucratic process is probably a sensible way. However, whether the swing to the other extreme will lead to a Chinese version of Stalinist bureaucratic socialism is a question worth pondering. We certainly do not believe that the alternatives to building socialism are so limited as to necessitate a choice between a Stalinist bureau-cratic system leading to a "forced" industrialization and a Radical Maoist voluntarist political approach leading to anarchistic counter-productive development. However, a cold fact seems to be that neither Marx nor Lenin nor Stalin nor probably even Mao can help the Modernistic Maoists very much to build a great modern society which is truly "Chinese" and "socialist" before the end of this century. And, after more than ten years of fruitless utopian engineering, the most urgent and serious task for the modernistic elites in China today is to have to think painfully anew of a road of transition from the "kingdom of necessity" to the "realm of liberty."

---

tion," in W. Bennis, Kenneth D. Benne and Robert Chin (eds.), *The Planning of Change*, 2nd edition (New York: Holt, Rinehart and Winston, 1969), p. 579.

[55]Cheng Háng-shéng, "A Discussion on Rampant Metaphysics," *Kuang Ming Daily*, March 29, 1977.

[56]Teng's Documents, *op. cit.*, p. 276.

CHAPTER EIGHT

A Summary Review

John F. Jones

Part of the difficulty in assessing China's development is a general problem involving the use of indicators. The road to integrated development needs milestones to mark the distance traveled. Crude economic indicators, such as GNP and per capita income, are insufficient when evaluating development, and even reliance on more refined industrial indices does not eliminate the danger of a one-sided, purely economic, evaluation. Indicators able to discern the social nuances of progress must supplement aggregative indices; such indicators would include urban and rural employment, change in levels of living, social mobility, the altered status of women, popular participation or the actual exclusion of some groups from economic and social progress.[1] But to evaluate social advancement, a yardstick is also necessary. What is needed are: indicators of distribution, including income distribution; indicators of qualitative factors, such as quality of education; and indicators of environmental conditions.[2] Ideally, the techniques of measuring these should be so refined as to provide a basis for typological analysis, and assist in cross-sectoral diagnosis.[3]

The task of measurement becomes still more complex when exploring socio-economic development at the local level. Here there is a tendency—reflected in the present volume's Guangdong commune studies, for instance—to describe particular programs as illustrations of widespread progress. The hypothesis, were it spelled out, would probably be that through the systematic examination and mapping of progress in specific villages, small towns and city

---

[1] John F. Jones, "Introduction to Development: An International Perspective," in John F. Jones and Rama S. Pandey (eds.), *Social Development: Conceptual, Methodological and Policy Issues* (London and New Delhi: Macmillan, in press).

[2] *Research Notes*, No. 4, United Nations Research Institute for Social Development, Geneva, 1974.

[3] See D. V. McGranahan, *et al.*, *Contents and Measurement of Socioeconomic Development* (New York: Praeger, 1972).

districts (or production teams, brigades and communes), it should be feasible to assess more accurately, and in a manner national surveys cannot, not only the social aspects of change but the interrelationship of the economic and social factors of development. A major deficiency of national planning has been the failure of national planning offices to obtain adequate information on what is actually happening in the country outside the capital, what changes are taking place in the villages and towns, who benefits from development, and so on.[4]

Those who advocate the collection at the local level of specific data on particular programs do so on the grounds that these are generally more amenable to collecting and reporting than are indicators of income and expenditure which have their own problems of definition and validation. Those who opt for national-type surveys, whether economic, political or social, clearly prefer more general, if crude, criteria of progress and reject the case approach of local studies. Since in the present situation of most Third World countries the impartial collection of socio-economic data at the local level is open to question and since national reporting systems are poor by Western standards, we are left with a choice of two defective sets of indicators or with attempting to combine the two.

In the case of China, the imperfections of the national reporting system and the imprecision of comparing one region or commune with another might provide an excuse, if one were needed, for avoiding any overall assessment of progress. Besides, selected studies of China's post-liberation years hardly justify a definitive statement on the degree of integrated development the People's Republic has achieved since 1949. Nonetheless, adhering to the general meaning of integrated development outlined in the Introduction, there seems enough evidence, both macro and micro, to draw some cautious conclusions about the nature of the country's development over the past three decades. It may be remembered that development is unified by being (to a greater or less degree depending on the actual implementation of policy) comprehensive, coordinated, integrated vertically and/or horizontally. If judgments on how far China has achieved a unified approach to development are ruled out, then impressions at least are unavoidable. The evidence does, at a minimum, suggest trends.

One of the most striking changes in post-1949 China was the extension of government and party organization from Peking throughout the country. Local government prior to the revolution meant county government. The CCP was, by and large, successful in integrating the country vertically. The vertical integration is very noticeable in China's industrialization, especially

[4]Wolf Scott, Helen Argalias and D. V. McGranahan, *The Measurement of Real Progress at the Local Level* (Geneva: United Nations Research Institute for Social Development, 1973), pp. 56-61.

immediately following the establishment of the People's Republic. Hsueh and Liu (ch. II) have documented the stress put on building up the heavy industries as a means of establishing the basic economic structure for production. This policy was later modified by a rejection of Soviet development strategies and by concentrating more on agriculture and small-scale industrial production. However, both policies—the early one-sided emphasis on heavy industry and the later "walking on two legs" formula—received their impetus and legitimacy from the party.

The success in vertical integration was not achieved without cost and has varied over the years. It took several years in the early 1950s for the government and the party to assert their control. Some of the factors to which Hsueh and Liu attribute China's success in industrialization—the rationalization of economic behavior by the collective forces, mass mobilization and better utilization of the labor force, the control of consumption and the effective channeling of savings into investment—were certainly imposed from above and resented by the masses at different times with varying degrees of hostility. During the Great Leap Forward and more especially during the Cultural Revolution, China was less vertically integrated than at other times. Official interpretations of the Cultural Revolution have changed since 1976. Initially seen as an immensely successful operation by the party to rid itself of "capitalist roaders," the movement is now seen as resulting in great disorder, which brought "calamity" to the Chinese people, and resulted in a "severe reversal" of the socialist revolution. Lin Piao and the Gang of Four took advantage of errors made in the party during this period to

> ... undermine the foundation of our socialist system, subvert the dictatorship of the proletariat, destroy the leadership of the Party, adulterate Marxism-Leninism-Mao Zedong Thought, and plunge China once again into the division and chaos abhorred by the people, into blood-baths and terror.[5]

During the Leap and the Cultural Revolution central planning suffered, and the disorder of the second period in particular led to local defiance of authority from 1966 to 1969. The revolutionary romanticism and mass activism of the Cultural Revolution were, according to King (ch. VII), based

[5] Yeh Chien-ying's speech to the Fourth Plenum of the Eleventh Central Committee of the CCP in *Beijing Review*, No. 40 (October 5, 1979), p.15. Likewise, Yeh Chien-ying has denounced the repression following the Hundred Flowers campaign, calling the 1957 attack on the rightists "impudent": "While it was necessary to counter the attack of a handful of bourgeois rightists, the mistake was made of broadening the scope of the struggle." In Yeh's speech to the Fourth Plenum of the Eleventh Central Committee of the CCP, *Beijing Review*, No. 40 (October 5, 1979), p. 14. The rightist labels are now gradually being removed. See Hua Kuo-feng's report to the Second Session of the Fifth National People's Congress, *Beijing Review*, No. 25 (June 22, 1979), p. 9.

upon anti-bureaucratism. It would follow, then, that the more recent rewriting of official history as well as the four modernizations mark—and mask—a de-radicalization of Maoism.

There is, however, a paradox in all of this. Even when vertical integration was at its weakest, horizontal integration was being strengthened in some important ways. The traditional horizontal integration of the countryside declined as a result of collectivization, marriage patterns, and the disappearance of the intermediate market towns (Jones and Burns, ch. I). In urban areas which obviously never possessed the rural network of relationships, it could be argued that relations between factories and residents' committees actually grew stronger through links with the party, despite periodic turmoil. In the countryside the party was also an integrating influence, to some extent countering the unfastening of close traditonal ties.

The commune movement which outlived both the passing of the Great Leap Forward and Cultural Revolution was perhaps Mao's most daring experiment in horizontal integration. The communes sought to combine the various functions of government administration, industry and commerce, agriculture, and the social services. How well they have done so has never been accurately assessed in a scientific manner for the country as a whole. But there are enough descriptive studies to suggest that some communes at least had remarkable success in multi-functional organization and operation. Small-scale projects which matched the capability of the commune at one and the same time improved material conditions and strengthened horizontal integration, as Y. K. Chan (ch. V) has indicated. The "sufficiently large" size of the commune population as well as the "higher degree of collective ownership" of the commune facilitated the comprehensive planning and implementation of projects. In carrying out projects, the commune formed a total political and social entity working under party guidance.

It is fairly clear that the commune system has had elements of both vertical and horizontal integration. Water conservancy, for instance, is both a local and central responsibility and demands teamwork at the grassroots level in addition to overall coordination, especially when large-scale projects are being attempted. The three-level system of collective ownership, responsibility and administration (communes, brigades, production terms), and the subordination of lower to higher level units favor comprehensive water conservancy schemes. While horizontal integration implies popular participation, it should not be forgotten that the coercive power existing within the three-level system plays its part in ensuring the mobilization of resources.

Development policies in China have in general been linked sequentially. Collectivization initiatives in rural areas coincided with similar moves in the cities. But some policies, such as communication, have not followed this general pattern. Urban communes, experimented with from 1958 to 1960, were quickly abandoned. Furthermore, from 1962 onwards, urban and rural policies were the subject of intense leadership disputes and their formulation and implementation were less well coordinated.

On the whole, however, the planned sequence of China's development can be perceived even when plans went awry and adjustments had to be made. Cheng (ch. VI) has argued that the direction of economic policy after the Cultural Revolution suggested a synthesis of elements of the Great Leap and concessions to the materialistic demands of peasants and workers. He would seem further to imply that even the post-1976 modernization was not entirely novel, since the broad outline of the modernization development strategy was confirmed at the Tenth Party Congress in 1973 and at the Fourth National People's Congress in 1974. If Dr. Cheng is correct in asserting that the political alarms and excursions of the years following the Cultural Revolution did not substantially alter the Chinese development strategy and that the Gang of Four never succeeded in formulating any credible alternative development strategy during this period, then of course China's socio-economic progress is remarkably unified in its sequence.

By and large, the leadership's problem-solving approach, its strategic orientation to development, has been an integrated one. There are, of course, fuzzy areas—notably the ambivalence of Chinese leaders towards material incentives and their on-again-off-again approval of limited private enterprise. Still, problems more often than not have been seen in their political, economic and social aspects, taken together, although one might question the hierarchy of values. Education, for instance, has generally been geared to serve the needs of the state. Rural education, as Ng (ch. III) has shown, has adapted its curriculum and its teaching methods to agriculture, economic productivity and commune life. China's leaders have also sought to use the schools to culti-vate the new "socialist man."

A comprehensive approach to service delivery is also noticeable in China's health care system. Lee and Tsui (ch. IV) demonstrate how the political-administrative structure of the commune has been utilized in the delivery of both preventive and curative health services. A regionalized health network exists which extends from the provincial and prefectural levels, through the county, and down to the commune, the brigade and the production team. This approach to health care is possible because rural institutions are them-selves comprehensive, incorporating economic, political and social functions. These institutions have permitted the development of health care, social welfare, housing and birth control policies in a relatively unified manner. The extension of electrification, irrigation and rural industry—in conjunction with the social services—is again evidence of integration. Precisely because commune organization is all-encompassing, it fosters comprehensive planning.

In the final analysis, integrated development means that policies are actually carried out. That there should be no hitch in plan implementation is almost too much to ask of any society, and China has failed on several occasions when the center's policies were obstructed, and unified implementation seriously undermined: first, during the setting-up of the higher-stage agricultural producers' cooperatives (HAPC's) in 1955-56; then, immediately preceding and during the Cultural Revolution when the "center" was speaking with several voices, and finally, during the 1973-76 struggle between Teng and Chiang Ch'ing and their respective supporters when again there was disunity within the leadership.[6]

After the Cultural Revolution, however, institutions were restored which facilitated the reintegration of central planning. Key decisions were again being taken in Peking and, after a brief debate, economic modernization and industrial growth were singled out as the chief priority. Especially after 1976, the leadership appeared to be united around these goals. Two significant events in the reintegration process were the Third Plenum of the Eleventh Central Committee, held in December 1978, and the subsequent second session of the Fifth National People's Congress in June 1979. On both occasions the stress was put on pragmatism (as Teng Hsiao-p'ing put it, "practice is the sole criterion of truth"), and thus exorcized for the moment at least the country's most radical ghosts. It was during the Fifth National People's Congress that Premier Hua Kuo-feng unveiled a new three-year program to "re-adjust, restructure, consolidate and improve" the national economy. The modernization of the economy is linked to an effort to raise the standard of living and provide both the urban and rural workers with higher incomes. How long China's renewed attempt to sustain its progress will remain on an even keel remains to be seen, but its success must depend on making all the factors of integrated development—the social no less than the economic and political —the object of policy.

---

[6]The Tien-an-man incident highlighted the division within the leadership in almost melodramatic fashion. The disturbance, originally declared "counter-revolutionary" by Chiang Ch'ing and her supporters (they blamed it on Teng Hsiao-p'ing and used it as one reason for his subsequent dismissal), has since been declared a "revolutionary" experience. Those arrested during the disturbance have been made "heroes of the April 5th Movement." See Communique of the Third Plenum of the Eleventh Central Committee on the CCP in Peking Review, No. 52 (December 29, 1978), p. 6.

Glossary

In the first part of the glossary, those words written in the text according to their popular English spelling and/or the Wade-Giles romanization system are given their Pinyin form that is now common on the mainland. In the second part of the glossary, Pinyin words found in the text are given their popular and/or Wade-Giles form.

I

	Popular and/or Wade-Giles spelling	Pinyin
安徽	Anhwei	Anhui
張春橋	Chang Ch'un-chiao	Zhang Chunqiao
廣州	Canton	Guangzhou
鄭州	Chengchow	Zhengzhou
成都	Chengtu	Chengdu
江青	Chiang Ch'ing	Jiangqing
周恩來	Chou En-lai	Zhou Enlai
重慶	Chungking	Chongqing
福州	Foochow	Fuzhou
河南	Honan	Henan
河北	Hopei	Hobei
華國鋒	Hua Kuo-feng	Hua Guofeng
湖南	Hunan	Hunan
湖北	Hupei	Hubei
甘肅	Kansu	Gansu
江蘇	Kiangsu	Jiangsu
江都	Kiangtu	Jiangdu
貴州	Kweichow	Guizhou
昆明	Kunming	Gunming
國民黨	Kuomintang	Guomindang
廣州	Kwangchow	Guangzhou
廣西	Kwangsi	Guangxi
貴陽	Kweiyang	Guiyang
李先念	Li Hsien-nien	Li Xiannian
遼寧	Liaoning	Liaoning
林彪	Lin Piao	Lin Biao

	Popular and/or Wade-Giles spelling	Pinyin
劉少奇	Liu Shao-ch'i	Liu Shaoqi
旅順	Lu-shun	Lushun
毛澤東	Mao Tse-tung	Mao Zedong
寧夏	Ninghsia	Ningxia
包頭	Paotow	Baotou
北京	Peking	Beijing
彭德懷	Peng Teh-huai	Peng Dehuai
西安	Sian	Xian
上海	Shanghai	Shanghai
山東	Shantung	Shandong
瀋陽	Shenyang	Shenyang
大寨	Tachai	Dazhai
大慶	Taching	Daqing
台北	Taipei	Taibei
台山	Taishan	Taishan
太原	Taiyuan	Taiyuan
大連	Talien	Dalian
鄧小平	Teng Hsiao-p'ing	Deng Xiaoping
鄧子恢	Teng Tzu-hui	Deng Zihui
天安門	T'ien-an-men	Tiananmen
天津	Tientsin	Tianjin
青海	Tsinghai	Qinghai
青島	Tsingtao	Qingdao
王洪文	Wang Hung-wen	Wang Hongwen
武漢	Wuhan	Wuhan
揚子	Yangtze	Yangzi
姚文元	Yao Wen-yuan	Yao Wenyuan
葉劍英	Yeh Chien-ying	Ye Jianying
余秋里	Yu Chiu-li	Yu Qiuli
元	*yuan*	*yuan*

II

	Pinyin	Popular and/or Wade-Giles spelling
安徽	Anhui	Anhwei
鞍山	Anshan	Anshan
北村（水閘）	Beicun	Pei Ts'un
茶坑（大隊）	Chakeng	Ch'a K'eng

	Pinyin	Popular and/or Wade-Giles spelling
長虹嶺	Chang Hongling	Ch'ang Hung-ling
成都昆明	Chengdu Kunming	Ch'eng-t'u K'un-ming
赤溪	Chixi	Ch'ih Hsi
冲蔞	Chonglou	Ch'ung Lou
大瀝	Dali	Ta Li
大隆洞	Dalongdong	Ta Lung-tung
大沙河	Dashahe	Ta-sha-ho
大圍	*dawei*	*ta-wei*
鄧小平	Deng Xiaoping	Teng Hsiao-ping
東甲	Dongjia	Tung-chia
東甲大圍	Dongjia Dawei	Tung-chia Ta-wei
都伏	Doufu	Tou Fu
斗山（公社）	Doushan	Tou Shan
端芬	Duanfen	Tuan Fen
恩平	Enping	En P'ing
峰火角	Fenghuojiao	Feng-huo-chiao
佛山	Foshan	Fo Shan
公路大圍	Gonglu Dawei	Kung-lu Ta-wei
掛鈎	*guagou*	*kua-kou*
廣東	Guangdong	Kwangtung
廣海	Guanghai	Kwanghai
廣州	Guangzhou	Canton
合山	Heshan	He-shan
環城	Huancheng	Huan Ch'eng
湖南	Hunan	Hunan
斤	*jin*	*chin*
錦江	Jin Jiang	Chin Chiang
九龍	Jiulong	Chiulung
開平	Kaiping	K'ai-p'ing
遼寧	Liaoning	Liaoning
林彪	Lin Biao	Lin Piao
里水	Lishui	Li Shui
羅崗	Luogang	Lo Kang
旅順	Lu-shun	Lu-shun
毛澤東	Mao Zedong	Mao Tse-tung
梅江	Mei Jiang	Mei Chiang
畝	*mu*	*mou*
南海	Nanhai	Nan Hai
三合海	Sanhehai	San-he-hai

	Pinyin	Popular and/or Wade-Giles spelling
沙口	Shakou	Sha K'ou
上海	Shanghai	Shaghai
瀋陽	Shenyang	Shenyang
台山	Taishan	T'ai Shan
潭江	Tan Jiang	T'an Chiang
天馬	Tianma	Tien Ma
圍	*wei*	*wei*
武漢	Wuhan	Wuhan
縣	*xian*	*hsien*
仙溪	Xianxi	Hsien Hsi
西江	Xi Jiang	Hsi Chiang
新會	Xinhui	Hsinhui
新興	Xinxing	Hsinhsing
鹽步	Yanbu	Yen Pu
鄭州	Zhengzhou	Chengchow
珠江	Zhu Jiang	Chu Chiang (Pearl River)

List of Contributors

John P. Burns, B.A. (*Oxford*), Ph.D. (*Columbia*) is Lecturer in Political Science, University of Hong Kong. His principal research interest is local Chinese politics since 1949, and he has contributed to various scholarly journals and books, including *China Quarterly* and the *Hong Kong Journal of Public Administration*.

Y. K. Chan, B.S.Sc. (*C.U.H.K.*), D.U. (*Bordeaux*) is Lecturer in Sociology and Project Associate of the Social Research Centre, The Chinese University of Hong Kong. His major research areas are demography, urban study and planning.

Joseph Y. S. Cheng, B.Soc.Sc. (*H.K.*), B.A. (*Well.*), Ph.D. (*Flinders*) is Lecturer in Government and Public Administration, The Chinese University of Hong Kong. He has been a commentator and columnist on international affairs and politico-economic developments in China, and has contributed to such journals as *Asia Quarterly*, *Journal of Contemporary Asia*, and *Asian Survey*.

T. T. Hsueh, B.A., M.A. (*Natnl. Taiwan*), Ph.D. (*Colorado*) is Lecturer in Economics, The Chinese University of Hong Kong. He was previously Associate Professor at National Taiwan University. His main publications include *An Econometric Model for Taiwan Economic Development*, 1971; and a Chinese translation with Translator's Note of Paul A. Samuelson's *Foundations of Economic Analysis*, 1974.

John F. Jones, B.A. (*Nat. Univ. Ireland*), M.S.W. (*Mich.*), M.A.P.A., Ph.D. (*Minn.*) is Professor and Chairman of the Social Work Department, The Chinese University of Hong Kong. Formerly, he was Dean of the School of Social Development, University of Minnesota. His publications include *Citizens in Service: Volunteers in Social Welfare during the Depression, 1929-41* (with John M. Herrick, 1976), *Social Welfare Administration* (in Chinese with Li Bik-chi, 1979), and *Education in Depth*, 1979.

Ambrose Y. C. King, B.A. (*Natnl. Taiwan*), M.A. (*Natnl. Chengchi*), M.A., Ph.D. (*Pitt.*) is Reader and Chairman of the Sociology Department, and Head of New Asia College, The Chinese University of Hong Kong. His publications include *The Historical Development of Chinese Democratic Thought* (in Chinese, 1966, with a revised edition in 1978) and *The Modernization of China and Intellectuals* (in Chinese, 1971).

Rance P. L. Lee, B.S.Sc. (*C.U.H.K.*), Ph.D. (*Pitt.*) is Senior Lecturer in Sociology and Director of the Social Research Centre, The Chinese University of Hong Kong. He is the author of numerous research monographs on social development, and is currently coordinator of the Guangdong rural communes study, "The Commune and Socio-economic Development in Communist China."

Pedro P. T. Ng, B.S.Sc. (*C.U.H.K.*), Ph.D. (*Harv.*) is Lecturer in Sociology, The Chinese University of Hong Kong. He has published research articles in a number of scholarly journals, including the *Cambridge Journal of Education*, *China Quarterly*, and *Modern China*.

W. Y. Tsui, B.S.Sc., M.Phil. (*C.U.H.K.*) is a researcher on health delivery systems in China. She was formerly a Teaching Assistant in Sociology at The Chinese University of Hong Kong, and a team member of the research project, "The Commune and Socio-economic Development in Communist China."

P. W. Liu, A.B. (*Princeton*), Ph.D. (*Stanford*) is Lecturer in Economics, The Chinese University of Hong Kong. He is engaged in research on the Chinese economy, as well as labor economics.

DATE DUE